HMH |

Practice and Homework Journal

Grade 2

Numbers to 20 and Data

Module 1—Fluency for Addition and Subtraction Within 20

Module 2—Equal Groups

Module 3—Data

Printed in the U.S.A.

ISBN 978-0-358-11100-9

6 7 8 9 10   0928   28 27 26 25 24 23 22 21

4500824211   C D E F G

Unit 2 Place Value

Unit 3 — Money and Tim

© Houghton Mifflin Harcourt Publishing Company

Unit 4 Two-Digit Addition and Subtraction

Unit 5 Three-Digit Addition and Subtraction

Unit 6 — Measurement: Length

© Houghton Mifflin Harcourt Publishing Company

Unit 7 Geometry and Fractions

© Houghton Mifflin Harcourt Publishing Company

Name _____

LESSON 1.1
More Practice/ Homework

ONLINE
Video Tutorials and
Interactive Examples

Use Doubles Facts to Add

Write an addition fact that shows the problem.
Then write a doubles fact that can help you
solve the problem. Solve.

1 (MP) **Use Structure** Colin has 7 marbles. He gets
6 more marbles from a friend. How many
marbles does Colin have now?

_____ + _____ = ■

doubles fact: _____ + _____ = _____

_____ marbles

2 Jake sees 5 crabs on the beach. Then he sees
6 more crabs. How many crabs does Jake see?

_____ + _____ = ■

doubles fact: _____ + _____ = _____

_____ crabs

(MP) **Use Repeated Reasoning** Write a doubles fact that
can help you find the sum. Write the sum.

3 1 + 2 = _____   doubles fact: _____ + _____ = _____

4 3 + 4 = _____   doubles fact: _____ + _____ = _____

5 **Math on the Spot** Mr. Norris wrote a doubles
fact. It has a sum greater than 6. The numbers
that he added are each less than 6. What fact
might he have written?

_____

Test Prep

6 Mr. Jamison catches 3 fish in the morning and 4 fish in the afternoon. Which doubles facts can help you find the number of fish Mr. Jamison catches? Choose the two correct answers.

○ $2 + 2 = 4$ ○ $5 + 5 = 10$

○ $3 + 3 = 6$ ○ $4 + 4 = 8$

For each addition fact, decide if you need 1 *more* or 1 *less* than the doubles sum. Circle the answer.

Fact	Doubles Fact	1 *more* or 1 *less*?	
7 $8 + 9 = \blacksquare$	$8 + 8 = 16$	1 more	1 less
8 $5 + 4 = \blacksquare$	$5 + 5 = 10$	1 more	1 less
9 $3 + 2 = \blacksquare$	$3 + 3 = 6$	1 more	1 less

Spiral Review

10 Kim has 6 cards. Her brother gives her 2 more cards. How many cards does she have now?

_____ cards

11 Solve. Then circle the related facts.

$5 + 0 =$ _____ $2 + 3 =$ _____ $3 + 2 =$ _____

Test Prep

4 Bart finds 9 shells on the beach. He gives 4 shells to a friend. How many shells does Bart have now? Fill in the bubble next to the correct answer.

○ 4   ○ 5   ○ 6

5 There are 10 cows in a field. 3 of the cows are brown. The rest of the cows are black and white. How many cows are black and white?

_____ black and white cows

Spiral Review

Write an addition fact to show the problem. Then write a doubles fact that can help you solve the problem. Solve.

6 Clive is making a poster. He has 5 markers in a box. He has 4 markers on his desk. How many markers does Clive have?

_____ + _____ = ■

doubles fact: _____ + _____ = _____

_____ markers

7 There are 7 green grapes and 8 red grapes in a bowl. How many grapes are there?

_____ + _____ = ■

doubles fact: _____ + _____ = _____

_____ grapes

LESSON 1.2
**More Practice/
Homework**

 ONLINE
Video Tutorials and
Interactive Examples

Develop Fluency with Addition Using Mental Strategies and Properties

(MP) **Attend to Precision** Solve. Show your work.

1 Alex has 3 pennies. Then he gets
   7 more pennies. How many pennies
   does Alex have now?

   _____ pennies

2 There are 5 green apples and 6 red apples
   in a basket. How many apples are in
   the basket?

   _____ apples

Solve.

3 **Math on the Spot** Sam painted 3 pictures.
   Ellie painted twice as many pictures as Sam.
   How many pictures did they paint?

   _____ pictures

(MP) **Use Repeated Reasoning** Find the sum.

4 $9 + 1 =$ _____   5 $6 + 8 =$ _____

6 $2 + 8 =$ _____   7 $9 + 0 =$ _____

Test Prep

8 Connie has 4 books. She buys 2 more books at the bookstore. How many books does Connie have now? Fill in the bubble next to the correct answer.

○ 2   ○ 6   ○ 7

9 Mr. Peterson drives 9 miles to the store.
Then he drives 3 more miles to work.
How many miles does he drive?

_____ miles

Spiral Review

Write an addition fact to show the problem.
Then write a doubles fact that can help you
solve the problem. Solve.

10 At a park, 6 dogs are sleeping and 5 dogs are
playing. How many dogs are there?

_____ + _____ = ■

doubles fact: _____ + _____ = _____

_____ dogs

11 There are 8 ducks in a pond. There are 9 ducks
in the grass. How many ducks are there?

_____ + _____ = ■

doubles fact: _____ + _____ = _____

_____ ducks

Name _____

Relate Addition and Subtraction

1 (MP) **Attend to Precision** Kathy has 6 crayons on her desk. Robert has 9 crayons on his desk. How many crayons do they have?

Write an addition fact. Complete the bar model. Write a related subtraction fact. Solve.

_____ + _____ = _____

_____ − _____ = _____

_____ crayons

2 (MP) **Reason** Explain how you used the bar model to write a related subtraction fact.

_____

_____

_____

_____

3 (MP) **Use Structure** Complete the addition facts and the bar model. Then complete the related subtraction facts.

$7 + 5 =$ _____

$5 + 7 =$ _____

$12 - 7 =$ _____

$12 - 5 =$ _____

Test Prep

4 Victoria has 17 ribbons. She has 8 red ribbons. The rest of the ribbons are green. How many green ribbons does Victoria have? Fill in the bubble next to the correct answer.

○ 8

○ 9

○ 10

Are the facts related facts? Write yes or no.

5 3 + 6 = 9

     9 − 6 = 3 _____

6 4 + 5 = 9

     5 − 4 = 1 _____

Spiral Review

7 Mrs. Dinson has 9 pencils on her desk. She has 3 pencils in a box. To find the number of pencils she has altogether, Mrs. Dinson writes 9 + 3 = 12. What other addition fact could Mrs. Dinson use?

_____

Develop Fluency with Subtraction Using Mental Strategies

(MP) **Use Structure** Write the subtraction fact. Then solve.

1 Jackie checks out 11 books from a library. She reads 7 of the books. How many books does Jackie have left to read?

_____ – _____ = _____

_____ books

---

2 Weston has 16 marbles in a jar. He takes 8 marbles out to play. How many marbles are in the jar now?

_____ – _____ = _____

_____ marbles

---

3 **Math on the Spot** Write the differences. Then write the next fact in the pattern.

$12 - 9 =$ _____

$13 - 9 =$ _____

$14 - 9 =$ _____

$15 - 9 =$ _____

_____

LESSON 1.5
**More Practice/
Homework**

ONLINE
Video Tutorials and
Interactive Examples

Use the Make a Ten Strategy to Add

(MP) Use Structure Make a ten to solve the problem. Show your work.

1 There are 4 bananas and 9 apples in a fruit bowl. How many pieces of fruit are in the bowl?

_____ pieces of fruit

2 There are 4 windows in a room. There are 7 windows in another room. How many windows are in both rooms?

_____ windows

(MP) Attend to Precision Make a ten to find the sum. Show your work. Write the sum.

3 $8 + 4 =$ _____

$10 +$ _____ $=$ _____

4 $8 + 3 =$ _____

$10 +$ _____ $=$ _____

5 $7 + 6 =$ _____

$10 +$ _____ $=$ _____

6 $5 + 9 =$ _____

$10 +$ _____ $=$ _____

Solve.

7 **Math on the Spot** There are 9 bees in a hive. How many more bees need to go in the hive for there to be 17 bees?

_____ more bees

Test Prep

8 Sam stacks 8 blocks. Then he adds 7 more blocks
to the stack. Which fact has the same sum as $8 + 7$?
Fill in the bubble next to the correct answer.

○ $10 + 5$

○ $10 + 6$

○ $10 + 7$

9 There are 4 red tulips and 9 white tulips in a vase.
Which facts show how you can make a ten to help
find the number of tulips in the vase? Choose the
two correct answers.

○ $5 + 5 = 10$ ○ $4 + 6 = 10$

○ $1 + 9 = 10$ ○ $7 + 3 = 10$

Spiral Review

Solve. Show your work.

10 Sara has 8 pages to color in one book. She has
9 pages to color in another book. How many
pages does she have to color? Write an addition
fact. Complete the bar model. Write a related
subtraction fact. Solve.

_____ = _____ + _____

_____ − _____ = _____

_____ pages

Name _____

LESSON 1.6
More Practice/ Homework

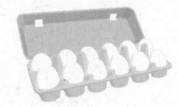
ONLINE
Video Tutorials and
Interactive Examples

Use a Tens Fact to Subtract

(MP) **Attend to Precision** Find the difference.
Show the tens fact you used.

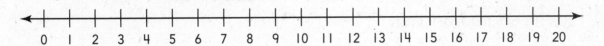

1. There are 16 toys in a toy box. Kylie takes
9 toys out of the toy box. How many toys
are in the toy box now? Show your work.

16 – _____ = _____

_____ toys

2. There are 12 eggs in a carton. Mrs. Kelly
uses 3 of the eggs. How many eggs are
in the carton now? Show your work.

12 – _____ = _____

_____ eggs

3. 13 – 6 = _____

10 – _____ = _____

4. 11 – 7 = _____

10 – _____ = _____

5. **Math on the Spot** Beth has a box of 18 crayons.
She gives 3 crayons to Jake and 7 crayons to
Wendy. How many crayons does Beth have now?

_____ crayons

Test Prep

6 There are 12 children playing tag. 7 children are tagged and now out of the game. Which has the same difference as 12 – 7? Fill in the bubble next to the correct answer.

○ 10 – 8

○ 10 – 7

○ 10 – 5

7 Which tens fact can help you find the difference? Fill in the bubble next to the correct answer.

14 – 6 = ■

○ 10 – 6 = _____

○ 10 – 2 = _____

○ 10 – 4 = _____

Spiral Review

Make a ten to solve the problem. Show your work.

8 Mr. Smith buys 6 muffins. Then he buys 7 more muffins. How many muffins does he have now?

_____ muffins

LESSON 1.7
**More Practice/
Homework**

⊙Ed **ONLINE**
Video Tutorials and
Interactive Examples

Add 3 Numbers Using Mental Strategies and Properties

(MP) **Use Structure** Write an addition fact to show the problem. Circle two addends to add first. Write the sum.

1 Andre sees 4 gray cars, 2 black cars, and 4 cars with a stripe. How many cars does Andre see?

_____ + _____ + _____ = _____

_____ cars

2 Mr. Daniels buys 3 stamps on Monday. He buys 4 stamps on Tuesday. He buys 6 stamps on Friday. How many stamps does Mr. Daniels buy?

_____ + _____ + _____ = _____

_____ stamps

3 **Math on the Spot** Nick, Alex, and Sophia eat 15 raisins in all. Nick and Alex each eat 4 raisins. How many raisins does Sophia eat?

_____ raisins

(MP) **Attend to Precision** Choose two addends to add first. Circle the addends. Write the sum.

4 $5 + 5 + 1 =$ _____   5 $2 + 7 + 3 =$ _____

Test Prep

6 There are three rows of chairs. In the first row, there are 4 chairs. In the second row, there are 4 chairs. In the last row, there are 6 chairs. Which can be used to find the total number of chairs? Choose the two correct answers.

○ $10 + 4 = 14$

○ $12 + 4 = 16$

○ $10 + 6 = 16$

○ $8 + 6 = 14$

7 What is the sum of $4 + 3 + 3$? Fill in the bubble next to the correct answer.

○ 7

○ 10

○ 11

Spiral Review

Solve. Show your work.

8 Kevin has a basket of 11 oranges. He eats 2 of the oranges. How many oranges are in the basket now?

_____ oranges

Identify Even and Odd Numbers

1 Marbles come in many colors. Most marbles are made from glass. Mr. Allen has 12 marbles. Does he have an even number or an odd number of marbles?

_____

(MP) **Use Tools** Show each number of objects using tools. Make pairs, or use a Hundred Chart to count by twos. Then write Even or Odd to describe the number of objects.

2 5 _____

3 6 _____

4 14 _____

5 18 _____

Test Prep

Fill in the bubble next to the correct answer.

6 Which is an even number?

○ 5   ○ 8   ○ 9

---

7 Which shows an odd number of strawberries?

○

○

○

Spiral Review

8 Complete the related facts.

$6 + 8 =$ _____ $14 - 6 =$ _____

$8 + 6 =$ _____ $14 - 8 =$ _____

LESSON 2.2
**More Practice/
Homework**

ONLINE
Video Tutorials and
Interactive Examples

Write Equations to Represent Even Numbers

1 (MP) **Use Repeated Reasoning** There are 20 basketballs and soccer balls in the youth center. There is the same number of each sports ball. How many of each sports ball is in the youth center? Write an addition equation to show the equal groups. Solve.

_____ = _____ + _____

_____ basketballs   _____ soccer balls

(MP) **Model with Mathematics** Write an addition equation to show the number as the sum of two equal addends.

2 12

_____ = _____ + _____

3 2

_____ = _____ + _____

4 16

_____ = _____ + _____

5 14

_____ = _____ + _____

Test Prep

Fill in the bubble next to the correct answer.

6 Which addition equation can you use to show the equal groups?

- ○ $4 = 2 + 2$
- ○ $10 = 5 + 5$
- ○ $12 = 6 + 6$

7 Which equation shows the number 4 as a sum of two equal addends?

- ○ $4 = 2 + 2$
- ○ $4 = 1 + 1 + 1 + 1$
- ○ $4 = 3 + 1$

Spiral Review

Make a ten to find the sum. Show your work.
Write the sum.

8 $8 + 6 =$ _____

$10 +$ _____ $=$ _____

9 $7 + 9 =$ _____

$10 +$ _____ $=$ _____

LESSON 2.3
**More Practice/
Homework**

☺Ed **ONLINE**
Video Tutorials and
Interactive Examples

Represent Equal Groups

Use tools or draw to solve.

1 (MP) **Use Structure** Natalie puts grapes in 5 rows.
She puts 5 grapes in each row. How many
grapes are there?

_____ grapes

Explain how you found the total number of grapes.

_____

_____

2 (MP) **Reason** Dylan puts his blocks in 4 rows. He puts
2 blocks in each row. How many blocks are there?

_____ blocks

Test Prep

Mila puts cubes in 4 rows. She puts 3 cubes in each row.

3 Which shows how Mila puts the cubes in equal rows? Fill in the bubble next to the correct answer.

○ (3 columns × 3 rows of cubes)

○ (4 columns × 2 rows of cubes)

○ (3 columns × 4 rows of cubes)

4 How many cubes does Mila put in rows?

_____ cubes

Spiral Review

Find the difference.

5 12 − 3 = _____

6 _____ = 15 − 9

7 _____ = 11 − 7

8 _____ = 14 − 6

Name _____

LESSON 2.4
**More Practice/
Homework**

ONLINE
Video Tutorials and
Interactive Examples

Add to Find the Total Number of Objects in Arrays

1 (MP) **Use Structure** Avery sees 2 rows of school buses. There are 5 buses in each row. How many buses are there?

Draw to show the school buses Avery sees.

Write an addition equation to solve the problem.

_____ + _____ = _____   _____ buses

2 (MP) **Model with Mathematics** Find the number of rows and the number of objects in each row. Then complete the addition equation to find the total.

_____ rows

_____ buttons in each row

_____ + _____ + _____ + _____ + _____ = _____

3 **Math on the Spot** There are 6 photos on the wall. There are 2 photos in each row. How many rows of photos are there?

_____ rows

Test Prep

4 Find the number of rows and the number of objects in each row. Then write an addition equation to find the total.

_____ rows

_____ stars in each row

_____ + _____ + _____ = _____

5 Tom draws these squares. How many squares does he draw? Fill in the bubble next to the correct answer.

○ 6

○ 8

○ 10

Spiral Review

Find the sum.

6 $6 + 3 =$ _____

7 _____ $= 9 + 2$

8 $7 + 6 =$ _____

9 _____ $= 8 + 6$

LESSON 2.5
**More Practice/
Homework**

 ONLINE
Video Tutorials and
Interactive Examples

Practice with Arrays

1 Isabel puts 5 rows of cups on a table. Each row has 2 cups. How many cups are there?

Draw to show how Isabel puts the cups on the table.

Write an addition equation to show how many cups there are.

_____ + _____ + _____ + _____ + _____ = _____

_____ cups

 Model with Mathematics Find the number of rows and the number of objects in each row. Then complete the addition equation to find the total.

2

_____ rows

_____ bananas in each row

_____ + _____ + _____ = _____

3

_____ rows

_____ hearts in each row

_____ + _____ + _____ + _____ = _____

Test Prep

Fill in the bubble next to the correct answer.

4 Carlos draws some soccer balls in rows. Which addition equation can you use to show the total number of soccer balls?

○ 2 + 2 + 2 = 6

○ 4 + 4 = 8

○ 4 + 4 + 4 = 12

5 There are 4 rows of peaches. There are 3 peaches in each row. How many peaches are there?

○ 7

○ 9

○ 12

Spiral Review

Choose two addends to add first. Circle the addends. Write the sum.

6 8 + 2 + 3 = _____

7 4 + 4 + 6 = _____

Name _____

LESSON 3.1
More Practice/ Homework

Ed **ONLINE**
Video Tutorials and
Interactive Examples

Collect and Record Data

1 (MP) **Use Tools** Take a survey of 10 classmates.
Ask them to choose their favorite color.
Complete the tally chart.

Favorite Color	
Color	Tally
green	
yellow	
blue	
red	

(MP) **Attend to Precision** Use the tally chart
to solve the problems.

2 How many classmates chose green or blue?

_____ classmates

3 Did more classmates choose red or blue?

_____

How many more?   _____ more classmates

4 How many fewer classmates chose green
than yellow?

_____ fewer classmates

Test Prep

Sandra took a survey of her classmates. She recorded their answers in the tally chart. Use the data from the tally chart to solve the problems. Fill in the bubble next to the correct answer.

Favorite Sandwich	
Sandwich	Tally
peanut butter	|||||
cheese	||||| ||||
turkey	||||| |||
tuna fish	||

5 Which sandwich did the most classmates choose?

○ peanut butter   ○ cheese   ○ turkey

6 How many more classmates chose turkey than tuna fish?

○ 2   ○ 4   ○ 6

Spiral Review

Find the sum.

7 _____ = 5 + 4

8 4 + 0 = _____

LESSON 3.2
**More Practice/
Homework**

ONLINE
Video Tutorials and
Interactive Examples

Interpret Picture Graphs

MP **Attend to Precision** Use the picture graph to solve the problems.

Number of Pencils										
Alana	✏	✏	✏	✏						
Teresa	✏	✏	✏	✏	✏	✏	✏			
John	✏	✏	✏	✏	✏					
Brad	✏	✏	✏	✏	✏	✏	✏	✏	✏	✏

Key: Each ✏ **stands for 1 pencil.**

1 Who has the most pencils? _____

2 How many pencils do Teresa and John have? _____ pencils

3 How many fewer pencils does Alana have than Teresa? _____ fewer pencils

4 How many more pencils does Brad have than John? _____ more pencils

5 **Math on the Spot** Mrs. Green has the same number of pencils as the four children. How many pencils does she have?

_____ pencils

Test Prep

Use the picture graph to solve. Fill in the bubble next to the correct answer.

Number of Stickers								
Paul	★	★	★	★	★	★		
Anna	★	★	★	★	★			
Beth	★	★	★	★	★	★	★	★
Lori	★	★	★					

Key: Each ★ stands for 1 sticker.

6 How many stickers do Anna and Beth have?

○ 5   ○ 8   ○ 13

7 How many fewer stickers does Lori have than Beth?

○ 3   ○ 5   ○ 6

Spiral Review

8 Circle all the sets of cubes that show an even number.

© Houghton Mifflin Harcourt Publishing Company

LESSON 3.3
**More Practice/
Homework**

ONLINE
Ed Video Tutorials and
Interactive Examples

Draw Picture Graphs to Represent Data

1 Nina and her friends picked apples. Draw a picture graph to show the data.

Nina picked 8 apples. Ian picked 9 apples.

Eva picked 2 apples. Tony picked 8 apples.

Number of Apples Picked											
Nina											
Eva											
Ian											
Tony											

Key: Each ◯ stands for 1 apple.

MP Use Structure Use the picture graph to solve the problems.

2 How many apples did Nina and Ian pick? _____ apples

3 Ian ate 2 of the apples he picked. How many apples does he have now? _____ apples

4 How many fewer apples did Eva pick than Nina? _____ fewer apples

5 How many more apples did Tony pick than Eva? _____ more apples

Test Prep

6 George made this picture graph.

Number of Flowers									
rose	◯	◯	◯	◯	◯	◯	◯	◯	◯
daisy	◯	◯	◯	◯	◯	◯	◯		
tulip	◯	◯	◯	◯	◯				
sunflower									

Key: Each ◯ stands for 1 flower.

Which group of pictures shows 9 sunflowers?
Fill in the bubble next to the correct answer.

○ | sunflower | ◯ ◯ ◯ ◯ ◯ ◯

○ | sunflower | ◯ ◯ ◯ ◯ ◯ ◯ ◯ ◯

○ | sunflower | ◯ ◯ ◯ ◯ ◯ ◯ ◯ ◯ ◯

Spiral Review

Write a doubles fact that can help you find the sum. Write the sum.

7 3 + 4 = _____

_____ + _____ = _____

8 9 + 8 = _____

_____ + _____ = _____

© Houghton Mifflin Harcourt Publishing Company

Name _____

LESSON 3.4
More Practice/ Homework

ONLINE
Video Tutorials and
Interactive Examples

Interpret Bar Graphs

MP **Attend to Precision** Use the bar graph to solve the problems.

1 Who read the most books?

_____

2 How many books did Rosa and Alex read?

_____ books

3 How many fewer books did Jim read than Rosa?

_____ fewer books

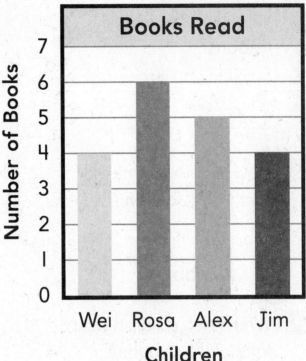

Books Read

Number of Books

Children
Wei Rosa Alex Jim

4 **Math on the Spot** Use the bar graph. Greg chose a place that has more votes than the aquarium and the museum together. Which place did Greg choose? _____

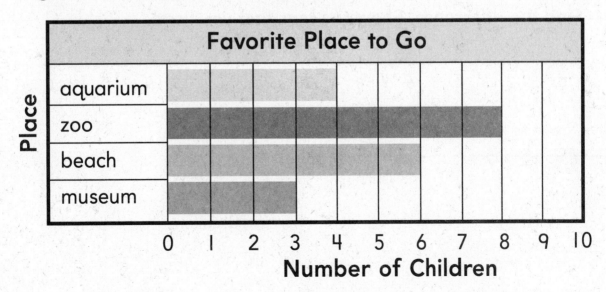

Favorite Place to Go

Place

aquarium
zoo
beach
museum

Number of Children
0 1 2 3 4 5 6 7 8 9 10

Test Prep

Use the bar graph to solve the problems.

5 Who won the fewest
ribbons?

_____

6 How many ribbons did
Jada and José win?

_____ ribbons

7 Which two children won a
total of 11 ribbons?

_____

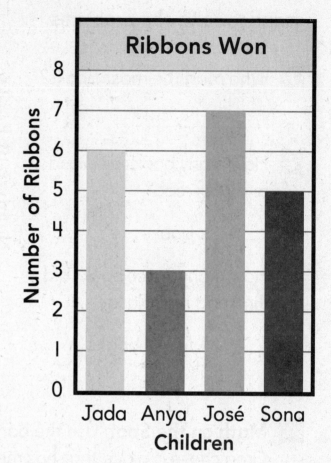

Ribbons Won

Number of Ribbons

8
7
6
5
4
3
2
1
0

Jada Anya José Sona

Children

Spiral Review

Find the difference. Show the tens fact you used.

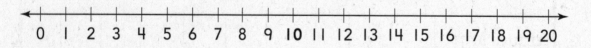

0 1 2 3 4 5 6 7 8 9 10 11 12 13 14 15 16 17 18 19 20

8 $13 - 7 =$ _____

$10 -$ _____ $=$ _____

9 $14 - 6 =$ _____

$10 -$ _____ $=$ _____

Draw Bar Graphs to Represent Data

1 There are 17 balloons in Kai's bag. There are 2 yellow, 4 green, and 3 pink balloons. The rest of the balloons are blue. Draw a bar graph to show the balloon colors.

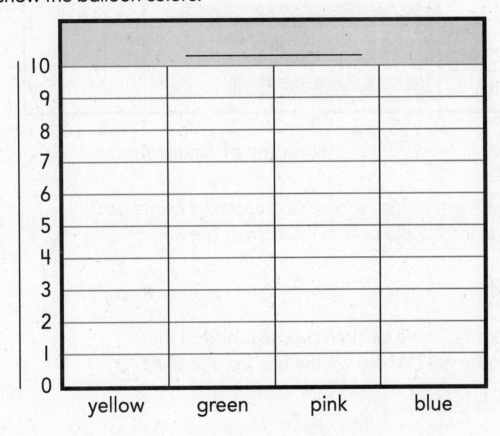

| | yellow | green | pink | blue |

_____

MP **Attend to Precision** Use the bar graph to solve the problems.

2 Which color balloon does Kai have the most of?

_____

3 How many yellow and green balloons does Kai have?

_____ yellow and green balloons

Test Prep

Use the bar graph to solve the problems.

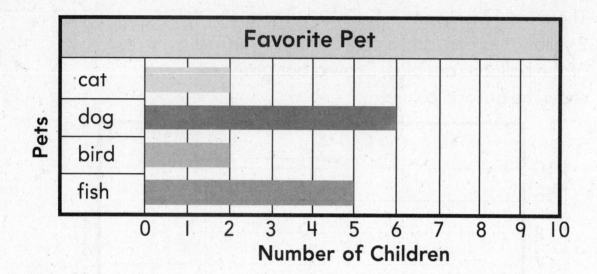

4 How many children chose dog as their favorite pet? Fill in the bubble next to the correct answer.

   ○ 2   ○ 5   ○ 6

5 What if 3 more children choose a bird as their favorite pet? Where will the bar for bird end?

_____

Spiral Review

6 Write the number of rows and the number of squares in each row. Then write an addition equation to find the total.

_____ rows

_____ squares in each row

_____ + _____ + _____ + _____ = _____

Group Tens as Hundreds

Solve.

1 (MP) **Use Repeated Reasoning** Jessie has 50 packages of sports cards. There are 10 sports cards in each package. How many sports cards does Jessie have?

Jessie has _____ sports cards.

2 **Math on the Spot** Wally has 400 cards. How many stacks of 10 cards can he make?

_____ stacks of cards

3 (MP) **Use Structure** Circle tens to make hundreds. Write the number three ways.

_____ tens

_____ hundreds

_____

Test Prep

4 Fill in the bubble next to the correct answer.
Tyesha has 20 flowerpots. She plants 10 seeds in
each pot. How many seeds does Tyesha have?

○ 100   ○ 200   ○ 300

5 There are 60 tens. Write how many hundreds.
Write the number.

_____ hundreds

_____

Spiral Review

6 Stacy has 9 books. Then she gets 4 more books.
How many books does Stacy have now?
Make a ten to solve the problem. Show your work.

$9 + 4 = \blacksquare$

_____   _____

$10 + \underline{\hspace{1.5cm}} = \underline{\hspace{1.5cm}}$

_____ books

7 Write the doubles fact that can help you find the
sum. Write the sum.

$8 + 9 = \underline{\hspace{2cm}}$

doubles fact: _____ + _____ = _____

Name _____

LESSON 4.2
**More Practice/
Homework**

ONLINE
Video Tutorials and
Interactive Examples

Understand Three-Digit Numbers

1 **Math on the Spot** Kendra has 120 stickers.
10 stickers fill a page. How many pages can
she fill?

Kendra can fill _____ pages.

2 Plants need space for their roots to grow. A
farmer plants 10 tomato plants in each row. She
plants 13 rows. How many tomato plants does the
farmer plant in all?

The farmer plants _____ tomato plants in all.

3 (MP) **Reason** Rachel and Jack collect marbles.
The marbles come in boxes of 10. Rachel has
10 boxes and Jack has 8 boxes. How many
marbles do Rachel and Jack have?

Rachel and Jack have _____ marbles.

4 (MP) **Use Repeated Reasoning** Circle tens to
make 1 hundred. Write the number three ways.

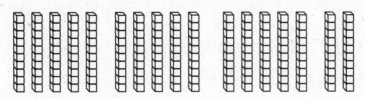

_____ tens

_____ hundred _____ tens

_____

Test Prep

5 Write the number three ways.

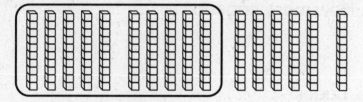

_____ tens

_____ hundred _____ tens

_____

6 There are 13 boxes of apples. There are 10 apples in each box. How many apples are there in all?

_____ apples

Spiral Review

7 There are 80 tens. Write how many hundreds. Write the number.

_____ hundreds

_____

8 Mrs. Vazquez buys 14 boxes of pencils. Each box has 10 pencils. How many pencils does Mrs. Vazquez buy?

_____ pencils

© Houghton Mifflin Harcourt Publishing Company

LESSON 4.3
**More Practice/
Homework**

ONLINE
Video Tutorials and
Interactive Examples

Represent Three-Digit Numbers

(MP) **Use Structure** Draw a quick picture. Write how many hundreds, tens, and ones. Solve.

1 Alisa needs 123 beads to design a shirt. A large bag holds 100 beads. A medium bag holds 10 beads. A small bag holds 1 bead. How many of each size bag of beads does Alisa need?

_____ hundred _____ tens _____ ones

Alisa needs _____ large bag, _____ medium bags,

and _____ small bags.

2 **Math on the Spot** How are the numbers 254 and 245 alike? How are they different?

_____

_____

_____

Write how many hundreds, tens, and ones.

3 989

_____ hundreds _____ tens _____ ones

4 607

_____ hundreds _____ tens _____ ones

Test Prep

5 Write how many hundreds, tens, and ones.

846

_____ hundreds _____ tens _____ ones

---

6 Fill in the bubble next to the correct answer.
A quick picture shows 3 hundreds, 2 tens, and
8 ones. Which number does the quick picture show?

○ 238

○ 328

○ 832

Spiral Review

7 There are 16 boxes of pencils. There are 10 pencils
in each box. How many pencils are there in all?

_____ pencils

8 Circle tens to make 1 hundred. Write the number
three ways.

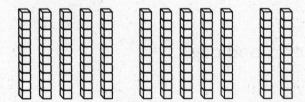

_____ tens

_____ hundred _____ tens

_____

LESSON 4.4
**More Practice/
Homework**

ONLINE
Video Tutorials and
Interactive Examples

Represent Numbers with Hundreds, Tens, and Ones

1 (MP) **Use Structure** Look at the blocks. Write how many hundreds, tens, and ones. Write the number two ways.

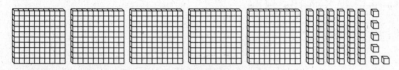

Hundreds	Tens	Ones

_____

_____ + _____ + _____

2 **Math on the Spot** A concrete model for my number has 9 ones blocks, 7 tens blocks, and 4 hundreds blocks. What number am I?

Write how many hundreds, tens, and ones.

Hundreds	Tens	Ones

Write the number as hundreds, tens, and ones.

_____ + _____ + _____

Write the number.

_____

Test Prep

3 Fill in the bubble next to the correct answer.
Which number is shown by the blocks?

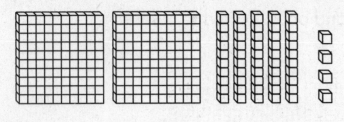

○ 245   ○ 254   ○ 452

4 Write the number 407 in another way.

_____ + _____ + _____

Spiral Review

5 Write the number that has the same value
as 14 tens.

_____

Circle *even* or *odd* to describe the number.

6 12   even   odd

7 15   even   odd

Find the sum.

8 8 + 2 = _____   **9** 5 + 0 = _____

10 _____ = 7 + 7   **11** _____ = 3 + 9

Name _____

LESSON 4.5
More Practice/ Homework

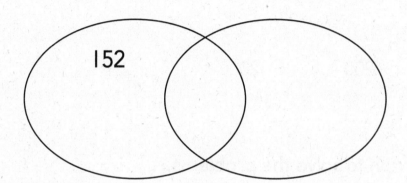ONLINE
Video Tutorials and
Interactive Examples

Place Value to 1,000

1 **Math on the Spot** Ty is making a Venn diagram. Where in the diagram should he write the other numbers?

Numbers with a 5 in the Tens Place　Numbers with a 2 in the Hundreds Place

152

| ~~152~~ |
| 215 |
| 454 |
| 257 |
| 352 |
| 205 |
| 250 |

2 Look at the underlined digit. Circle the value.

56<u>4</u>	4 ones	4 tens	4 hundreds
3<u>7</u>2	7	70	700
<u>8</u>35	8 ones	8 tens	8 hundreds
<u>1</u>,000	10	100	1,000

3 (MP) **Reason** Write the three-digit number that answers Sam's riddle.

• My hundreds digit and ones digit are the same.

• The value of my tens digit is 50.

• The value of my ones digit is 3.

_____

Test Prep

4 Write how many tens are in the number 179.

_____ tens

5 Fill in the bubble next to the correct answer.
Which tells the value of the underlined digit?

2̲45

○ 2,000   ○ 200   ○ 20

Spiral Review

Use the picture graph to solve the problems.

6 How many more children chose purple than blue?

_____ more children

Favorite Color							
blue	☺	☺	☺	☺	☺		
purple	☺	☺	☺	☺	☺	☺	☺
green	☺	☺	☺	☺			

Key: Each ☺ stands for 1 child.

7 How many children chose blue or green?

_____ children

8 Which two colors were chosen by a total of 9 children?

_____

9 Circle all of the numbers that are even.

12   7   5   10

Name _____

LESSON 5.1
More Practice/ Homework

ONLINE
Video Tutorials and
Interactive Examples

Use Expanded Form

1 **Open Ended** Nate sees toys at the toy store. He sees more than 200 toys, but fewer than 300. How many toys could Nate see? Draw to show the number. Write the number in different ways.

Write the number as hundreds, tens, and ones.

_____ hundreds _____ tens _____ ones

Write the number in expanded form.

_____ + _____ + _____

Nate sees _____ toys.

2 **(MP)** **Use Structure** Eric sees 146 marbles. Write the number of marbles in expanded form.

_____ + _____ + _____

3 Write the number 579 as hundreds, tens, and ones.

_____ hundreds _____ tens _____ ones

4 Write the number 579 in expanded form.

_____ + _____ + _____

Test Prep

5 There are 314 second graders. Use the quick picture to help you write the number of children in different ways.

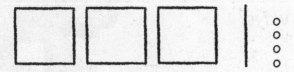

Write the number as hundreds, tens, and ones.

_____ hundreds _____ ten _____ ones

Write the number in expanded form.

_____ + _____ + _____

6 Write the number 547 in expanded form.

_____ + _____ + _____

Spiral Review

7 Find the number of rows and the number of circles in each row. Then write the addition equation to find the total.

●●●●●●   _____ rows

●●●●●●   _____ circles in each row

●●●●●●

_____ + _____ + _____ = _____

8 Circle all of the even numbers.

8   5   9   4

Name _____

LESSON 5.2
**More Practice/
Homework**

ONLINE
Ed Video Tutorials and
Interactive Examples

Use Number Names

1 There are 183 ants in the anthill.
Draw a quick picture to help you write
the number name.

_____

2 **Math on the Spot** Alma counts five hundred
twenty-four leaves. Which is another way to write
this number? Circle the correct answer.

$5 + 2 + 4$

$500 + 20 + 4$

$500 + 2 + 4$

MP **Use Structure** Draw a quick picture. Then write
the number name or the number.

3 116

4 three hundred twenty-seven

Test Prep

5 There are 192 snails in the park. Use the quick picture to help you write the number name.

_____

6 Write three hundred eleven using numbers.

_____

7 Write the number name for 516.

_____

Spiral Review

Use the bar graph to solve the problems.

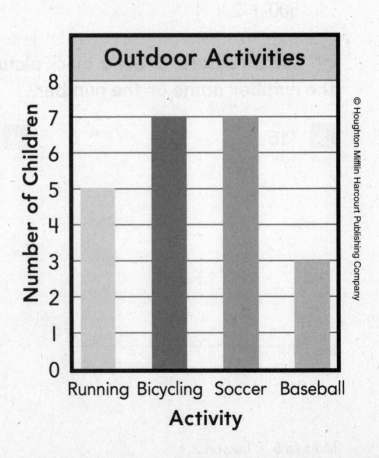

8 How many children like soccer or baseball?

_____ children

9 How many more children chose running than baseball?

_____ more children

LESSON 5.3
**More Practice/
Homework**

ONLINE
Video Tutorials and
Interactive Examples

Different Ways to Write Numbers

1 A bird uses four hundred thirty-five sticks
to build a nest. Write the number in
different ways.

_____ hundreds _____ tens _____ ones

_____ + _____ + _____

_____

---

2 **Math on the Spot** Ellen used these blocks to
show 547. What is wrong? Cross out blocks and
draw quick pictures for missing blocks.

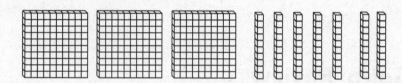

MP **Use Repeated Reasoning** Write the number two
hundred eighteen in different ways.

3 Write the number as hundreds, tens, and ones.

_____ hundreds _____ ten _____ ones

4 Write the number in expanded form.

_____ + _____ + _____

5 Write the number.

_____

Test Prep

6 Write the number five hundred seventeen in different ways.

_____ hundreds _____ ten _____ ones

_____ + _____ + _____

_____

7 Which shows the number seven hundred sixty-three? Fill in the bubble next to the correct answer.

○ 376

○ 736

○ 763

Spiral Review

8 Circle tens to make 1 hundred. Write the number three ways.

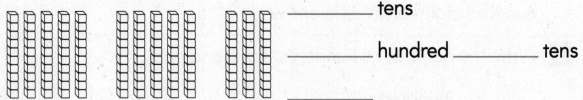

_____ tens

_____ hundred _____ tens

_____

9 Find the difference. Show the tens fact you used.

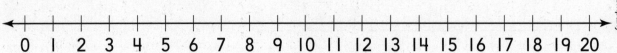

14 − 5 = _____

10 − _____ = _____

LESSON 5.4
**More Practice/
Homework**

ONLINE
Video Tutorials and
Interactive Examples

Different Ways to Show Numbers

1 (MP) **Reason** A library has 144 books. A long shelf can fit 100 books. A short shelf can fit 10 books. The books that are left over can be put in a bin. Draw two ways to sort books on a shelf.

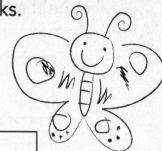

| | |
| | |

2 Look at your first drawing. Write the hundreds, tens, and ones.

_____ hundred _____ tens _____ ones

3 Look at your second drawing. Write the hundreds, tens, and ones.

_____ hundreds _____ tens _____ ones

4 **Math on the Spot** Marbles are sold in boxes, bags, or as leftover marbles. Each box has 10 bags of marbles in it. Each bag has 10 marbles in it. Draw quick pictures to show two ways to buy 246 marbles.

| | |
| | |

Test Prep

5 Use the two quick pictures for the number 156 to help you write the number of hundreds, tens, and ones in two ways.

First drawing: _____ hundred _____ tens _____ ones

Second drawing: _____ hundreds _____ tens _____ ones

Spiral Review

6 Cam asked his classmates to chose their favorite animal. 6 children chose cats. 7 children chose dogs. 1 child chose birds. 3 children chose fish. Draw a bar graph to show the data.

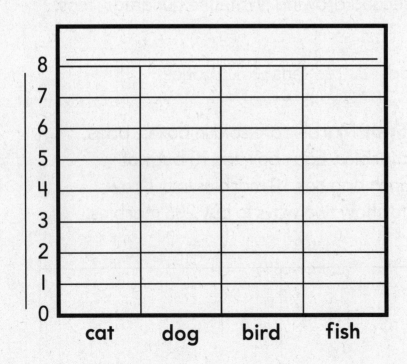

_____

LESSON 5.5
**More Practice/
Homework**

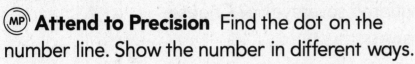

ONLINE
Video Tutorials and
Interactive Examples

Read, Write, and Show Numbers

(MP) **Attend to Precision** Find the dot on the number line. Show the number in different ways.

300   305   310   315   320   325   330   335   340   345   350

1 Write the number name.

_____

2 Draw a quick picture for the number.

3 Write the number in expanded form.

_____ + _____ + _____

4 Write the number.

_____

(MP) **Use Structure** Write the number six hundred fifteen in different ways.

5 Write the number as hundreds, tens, and ones.

_____ hundreds _____ ten _____ ones

6 Write the number in expanded form.

_____ + _____ + _____

7 Write the number.

_____

Test Prep

8 Which show four hundred seventy-five? Choose the two correct answers.

○ 457

○ 4 hundreds 7 tens 5 ones

○ 400 + 70 + 5

○ 700 + 40 + 5

9 Write two hundred sixteen in hundreds, tens, and ones and in expanded form. Then write the number.

_____ hundreds _____ ten _____ ones

_____ + _____ + _____

_____

Spiral Review

10 Find the number of rows and the number of squares in each row. Then write the addition equation to find the total.

_____ rows

_____ squares in each row

_____ + _____ + _____ = _____

11 Write a doubles fact that can help you find the sum. Write the sum.

5 + 4 = _____

doubles fact: _____ + _____ = _____

© Houghton Mifflin Harcourt Publishing Company

Name _____

LESSON 6.1
**More Practice/
Homework**

ONLINE
Video Tutorials and
Interactive Examples

Count Within 1,000

1 (MP) **Use Structure** A banana tree has 80 ripe bananas. Each day, 10 more bananas become ripe. Count by tens. How many bananas are ripe after 5 days?

80, _____, _____, _____, _____, _____

_____ bananas are ripe after 5 days.

2 (MP) **Use Tools** George counts by tens. He starts at 750. Look at the numbers. Circle the numbers George says.

| 755 | 690 | 760 | 795 | 780 | 810 |

(MP) **Reason** Count by fives.

3 265, 270, 275, _____, _____, _____

4 575, 580, 585, _____, _____, _____

(MP) **Use Repeated Reasoning** Count by tens.

5 860, 870, 880, _____, _____, _____

(MP) **Attend to Precision** Count by hundreds.

6 210, 310, 410, _____, _____, _____

Test Prep

7 Ben counts by fives, starting at 620. Sort the numbers to show Ben's counting pattern.

| 645 | 630 | 640 | 635 | 625 |

620, _____, _____, _____, _____, _____

Fill in the bubble next to the correct answer.

8 Which set of numbers shows counting by tens?

○ 380, 480, 580

○ 280, 380, 480

○ 360, 370, 380

---

9 Which set of numbers shows counting by hundreds?

○ 600, 700, 800

○ 680, 690, 700

○ 685, 690, 695

Spiral Review

10 Draw a quick picture for the number 420.

LESSON 6.2
**More Practice/
Homework**

ONLINE
Video Tutorials and
Interactive Examples

Add and Subtract 10 or 100

1 **(MP) Use Structure** There are 118 books on a shelf. A teacher takes 10 books off the shelf. How many books are on the shelf now? Explain.

_____

_____

_____

2 **(MP) Reason** Juan's book has 248 pages. Juan's book has 10 more pages than Kevin's book. How many pages are in Kevin's book?

_____ pages

3 **(MP) Use Repeated Reasoning** Use the number in the chart. Write three more numbers. Make each number 100 less than the number before.

Hundreds	Tens	Ones
5	7	6

_____ , _____ , _____

(MP) Attend to Precision Write the number.

4 100 less than 935 _____

5 10 more than 241 _____

6 100 more than 85 _____

7 10 less than 453 _____

Test Prep

8 Julian has 353 crayons. He loses 10 crayons. How many crayons does he have now?

_____ crayons

9 There are 482 stickers in the book. Then 100 stickers are added to the book. How many stickers are in the book now? Fill in the bubble next to the correct answer.

○ 483

○ 492

○ 582

Spiral Review

10 Write the number four hundred twenty-six in different ways.

_____ hundreds _____ tens _____ ones

_____ + _____ + _____

_____

LESSON 6.3
**More Practice/
Homework**

ONLINE
Video Tutorials and
Interactive Examples

Identify and Extend Number Patterns

1 There are 837 leaves on a plant. Each month, 100 leaves fall off. Complete the pattern to show how many leaves there are after each month.

837, _____, _____, _____, _____

Explain how you completed the pattern.

_____

_____

2 (MP) **Use Tools** What is the next number in the pattern?

453, 463, 473, 483, _____

(MP) **Attend to Precision** Complete the pattern.

3 180, 170, 160, _____, _____, _____, _____

4 899, 799, 699, _____, _____, _____, _____

5 305, 405, 505, _____, _____, _____, _____

6 575, 585, 595, _____, _____, _____, _____

7 719, 619, 519, _____, _____, _____, _____

Test Prep

8 Choose two numbers from the list to complete the pattern.

280, _____, 300, 310, _____, 330

270	320
290	340
305	350

---

9 Which is the next number in the pattern? Fill in the bubble next to the correct answer.

617, 517, 417, _____

○ 416

○ 407

○ 317

Spiral Review

10 Draw a quick picture and write the number name for 511.

LESSON 6.4
**More Practice/
Homework**

ONLINE
Video Tutorials and
Interactive Examples

Compare Three-Digit Numbers

1 (MP) **Attend to Precision** Mr. Wynn sells fruits and vegetables at his store. He sells 105 apples and 150 carrots on Monday. Does he sell more apples or carrots? Show each number. Compare the numbers to solve.

Mr. Wynn sells more _____ than _____.

2 (MP) **Use Tools** Molly's puzzle has 125 pieces. Sam's puzzle has 160 pieces. Whose puzzle has fewer pieces? Show each number. Compare the numbers to solve.

_____ puzzle has fewer pieces.

(MP) **Reason** Compare. Circle the number that is less.

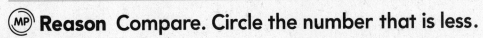

3 174   184   **4** 548   549

5 387   287   **6** 811   801

Test Prep

7 Kenny has 246 stamps. Sara has fewer stamps than Kenny. How many stamps might Sara have? Choose the two correct answers.

○ 174

○ 235

○ 247

○ 384

8 A necklace has 520 blue beads and 730 red beads. Which sentence is true? Fill in the bubble next to the correct answer.

○ There are more red beads than blue beads.

○ There are more blue beads than red beads.

○ There are fewer red beads than blue beads.

Spiral Review

Write the number in expanded form.

9 258 _____ + _____ + _____

10 183 _____ + _____ + _____

11 362 _____ + _____ + _____

12 414 _____ + _____ + _____

Name _____

LESSON 6.5
**More Practice/
Homework**

ONLINE
Video Tutorials and
Interactive Examples

Use Symbols to Compare Numbers

1 **Math on the Spot** Mrs. York has 400 red
stickers, 50 blue stickers, and 6 green stickers.
Mr. Reed has 438 stickers. Who has more stickers?
Write each number.

Hundreds	Tens	Ones

Write >, <, or = to compare the numbers.

456 ◯ 438

_____ has more stickers.

2 **Open Ended** Write a three-digit number that makes
the comparison true.

526 < _____

(MP) **Reason** Write >, <, or = to compare the numbers.

3 352 ◯ 352

4 400 ◯ 800

5 179 ◯ 169

6 632 ◯ 638

7 263 ◯ 263

8 307 ◯ 285

9 704 ◯ 714

10 550 ◯ 505

Test Prep

11 A store sells 105 shirts and 113 pants. Does the store sell more shirts or more pants? Compare the numbers to solve.

_____ ◯ _____

The store sells more _____.

12 Which numbers would make the comparison true? Choose the two correct answers.

_____ < 834

◯ 814   ◯ 824   ◯ 834   ◯ 844

13 Becky has more shells than Jordan. If Jordan has 427 shells, how many shells does Becky have? Fill in the bubble next to the correct answer.

◯ 568   ◯ 418   ◯ 399

Spiral Review

14 Look at the underlined digit. Circle the value.

43<u>5</u>	5 hundreds	5 tens	5 ones
7<u>6</u>3	6 hundreds	6 tens	6 ones
<u>2</u>18	2 hundreds	2 tens	2 ones

LESSON 7.1
**More Practice/
Homework**

⊙Ed **ONLINE**
Video Tutorials and
Interactive Examples

Relate Place Value to Coins

1 (MP) **Use Structure** Mark uses 4 dimes and
3 pennies to buy a pencil. Show the coins
in the chart below.

Tens	Ones

Write the number of tens and ones. Then find the
total value of Mark's coins.

_____ tens   _____ ones

_____ ¢

---

2 (MP) **Reason** What is the total value of these coins?
Explain.

_____

_____

_____

Test Prep

Use these coins to answer the questions.
Fill in the bubble next to the correct answer.

3 How many tens and ones are shown by the coins?

○ 4 tens 4 ones

○ 4 tens 3 ones

○ 3 tens 3 ones

4 What is the total value of the coins?

○ 33¢

○ 34¢

○ 43¢

Spiral Review

5 Count by fives.

35, 40, 45, _____, _____, _____, _____

Count by tens.

6 40, 50, 60, _____, _____, _____, _____

7 20, 30, 40, _____, _____, _____, _____

Name _____

LESSON 7.2
More Practice/ Homework

 ONLINE
Video Tutorials and
Interactive Examples

Identify and Find the Value of Coins

1 (MP) **Attend to Precision** Kevin uses these coins to buy a toy car. What is the total value of Kevin's coins? Explain.

_____

_____

_____

2 (MP) **Use Structure** Count on to find the total value.

_____ ¢, _____ ¢, _____ ¢, _____ ¢, _____ ¢, _____ ¢, _____ ¢

3 **Open Ended** Nikki wants to buy a ball for 82¢. What coins can she use to buy the ball? Draw to show your answer.

Test Prep

Fill in the bubble next to the correct answer.

4 Which shows how to count to find the total value
of the coins?

○ 25¢, 50¢, 60¢, 70¢, 75¢, 80¢, 85¢

○ 30¢, 40¢, 50¢, 60¢, 65¢, 70¢, 71¢

○ 25¢, 35¢, 45¢, 55¢, 60¢, 65¢, 70¢

5 What is the total value of the coins?

○ 62¢   ○ 72¢   ○ 81¢

Spiral Review

Write the number.

6 10 more than 439 is _____.   **7** 100 more than 578 is _____.

8 10 less than 213 is _____.   **9** 100 less than 825 is _____.

LESSON 7.3
**More Practice/
Homework**

ONLINE
Video Tutorials and
Interactive Examples

Compute the Value of Coin Combinations

1 (MP) **Attend to Precision** Bryan uses these coins to buy a bookmark. What is the total value of the coins? Draw to show your work.

_____

2 (MP) **Construct Arguments** Explain how you solved Problem 1.

_____

_____

_____

_____

3 (MP) **Use Repeated Reasoning** Rosa has these coins. What is the total value of her coins?

_____

Test Prep

Use these coins to answer the questions.

4 Which drawing shows the coins in order from greatest value to least value? Fill in the bubble next to the correct answer.

○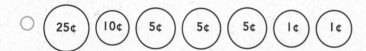

○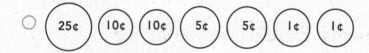

○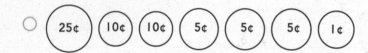

5 What is the total value of the coins? _____

Spiral Review

Write >, <, or = to compare the numbers. Solve.

6 A book about animals has 146 pages. A book about sports has 128 pages. Which book has fewer pages?

146 ◯ 128

The book about _____ has fewer pages.

LESSON 7.4
**More Practice/
Homework**

Ed **ONLINE**
Video Tutorials and
Interactive Examples

Show Amounts in Different Ways

1 Joey wants to buy a banana for 25¢. He
only has nickels. How many nickels have
the same total value as 1 quarter, or 25¢?
Draw to solve.

_____ nickels

2 (MP) **Use Tools** Tara finds 15¢. Draw coins to show two
ways to make 15¢.

3 (MP) **Attend to Precision** Nick buys an eraser for 20¢.
Draw coins to show two ways to make 20¢.

Test Prep

4 Which drawing shows coins with a total value of 5¢? Choose the two correct answers.

○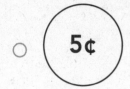

○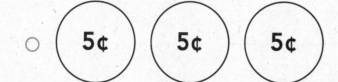

○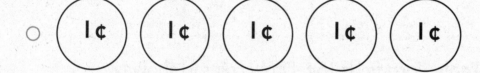

○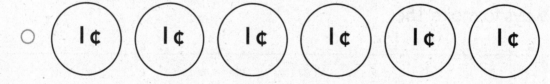

5 Which coin has the same value as 25 pennies?
Fill in the bubble next to the correct answer.

○ a nickel   ○ a dime   ○ a quarter

Spiral Review

Write >, <, or = to compare the numbers.

6 564 ◯ 562   **7** 735 ◯ 735

8 902 ◯ 920   **9** 804 ◯ 840

© Houghton Mifflin Harcourt Publishing Company

LESSON 8.1
**More Practice/
Homework**

ONLINE
Video Tutorials and
Interactive Examples

Relate the Value of Coins to One Dollar

1 (MP) **Reason** Harold has 4 quarters. Does he have $1.00? Explain.

_____

2 (MP) **Attend to Precision** Kendra needs $1.00 to buy a bouncy ball. She has 73¢. What coins does she need to add to her 73¢ to buy the bouncy ball?

Kendra needs _____ pennies, _____ nickel,

and _____ dimes.

3 (MP) **Reason** Adam wants to buy his sister a teddy bear. The teddy bear costs $1.00. He has 64¢. What coins does he need to buy the teddy bear? Explain.

_____

_____

4 (MP) **Use Tools** Sofia wants to buy a whistle for $1.00. She has 22¢. What coins does she need to buy the whistle? Draw the coins she needs to make $1.00.

Test Prep

5 Which group of coins has a value of $1.00?
Fill in the bubble next to the correct answer.

Spiral Review

6 Sarah buys a bookmark for 25¢. How many nickels
have the same total value as 25¢? Draw to solve.

_____ nickels

7 What is the total value of these coins?

_____

Name _____

LESSON 8.2
More Practice/ Homework

ONLINE
Video Tutorials and
Interactive Examples

Compute the Value of Dollar Combinations

1 (MP) **Use Structure** Mrs. Nance has one $20 bill, two $10 bills, one $5 bill, and three $1 bills. How much money does Mrs. Nance have?

Mrs. Nance has _____.

2 (MP) **Use Tools** Steve counts the money he saved. Count on to find how much money Steve saved.

_____, _____, _____, _____, _____, _____

Steve saved $ _____.

3 (MP) **Attend to Precision** Ms. Mons has one $20 bill, two $5 bills, and nine $1 bills. What bills could she add to make $60?

_____

_____

_____

Test Prep

Fill in the bubble next to the correct answer.

4 Which set of bills shows $42?

○

○

○

---

5 Isaiah saves money to buy a football.
How much money does Isaiah save?

○ $21   ○ $20   ○ $16

Spiral Review

6 Mike wants to buy a beach ball for $1. He has 65¢.
Draw the coins Mike needs to make $1.00.

Name _____

LESSON 8.3
**More Practice/
Homework**

ONLINE
Video Tutorials and
Interactive Examples

Solve Problems Involving Money

1 (MP) **Attend to Precision** Markus has one
$10 bill, three $5 bills, and one $1 bill. Count
on to find how much money Markus has.

_____, _____, _____, _____, _____

Markus has _____.

2 (MP) **Attend to Precision** Nina saves 43¢. What are
three different coin combinations Nina could have?

_____

_____

_____

3 (MP) **Reason** Kamal has one $10 bill, one $5 bill, and
four $1 bills. He wants to buy a basketball for $25.
Count on to find how much money Kamal has. Does
he have enough money to buy the basketball? Explain.

_____, _____, _____, _____, _____, _____

_____

_____

4 There is a different quarter for each of the 50 states in
the United States. Delaware was the first state to get
its own quarter. Anna has three state quarters. Her
brother gives her one more state quarter. How much
money does Anna have?

Anna has _____.

Test Prep

5 Charlie has 2 quarters, 2 dimes, and 5 pennies. Which combination of coins has the same total value? Fill in the bubble next to the correct answer.

   ○ 4 quarters

   ○ 7 dimes and 1 nickel

   ○ 2 quarters, 2 dimes, and 1 penny

6 Nadine has one $5 bill. Diana has five $1 bills. Who has more money? Explain.

_____

_____

Spiral Review

7 Jordan wants to buy a baseball for $1. He has 80¢. Draw the coins Jordan needs to buy the baseball.

8 Mrs. Seles has one $20 bill, two $10 bills, one $5 bill, and two $1 bills. Count on to find how much money she has.

_____ , _____ , _____ , _____ , _____ , _____

Mrs. Seles has _____.

LESSON 9.1
**More Practice/
Homework**

ONLINE
Video Tutorials and
Interactive Examples

Tell and Write Time to 5 Minutes

(MP) Use Structure Look at the time. Draw clock
hands to show the same time.

1 | 7:25

2 | 3:30

(MP) Attend to Precision Look at the clock hands.
Write the time.

3

4

5 **(MP) Use Tools** The clock shows what time Jorge gets
on the bus. Look at the time. Draw the clock hands to
show the same time.

8:25

Test Prep

Look at the clock hands. Write the time.

6

7

8

9

Spiral Review

10 Write the number name for 536.

_____

11 Write an addition equation
to find the total number
of marbles.

_____ + _____ + _____ = _____

Name _____

LESSON 9.2
**More Practice/
Homework**

Ed **ONLINE**
Video Tutorials and
Interactive Examples

Different Ways to Tell and Write Time

 **Attend to Precision** Draw the clock hands to show the time. Write the time.

1 Kirk goes to school at half past 9.

2 Tim reads a book until quarter past 6.

3 15 minutes after 7

4 half past 10

5 5 minutes after 12

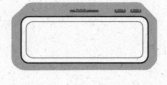

Test Prep

6 What time does the clock show? Fill in the bubble next to the correct answer.

○ 20 minutes past 11

○ 25 minutes past 11

○ half past 11

7 How can you say the time? Fill in the blanks to show how.

_____ minutes after _____   half past _____

Spiral Review

8 What is the value of the digit 5 in the number 540?

_____

9 Write a doubles fact that can help you find the sum. Write the sum.

7 + 8 = _____

doubles fact: _____ + _____ = _____

Name _____

LESSON 9.3
**More Practice/
Homework**

 **ONLINE**
Video Tutorials and
Interactive Examples

Practice Telling and Writing Time

 Use Structure Write the time in different ways.

1

_____ : _____

_____ past _____

_____ minutes after _____

2

_____ : _____

_____ past _____

_____ minutes after _____

3

_____ : _____

_____ minutes after _____

4

_____ : _____

_____ minutes after _____

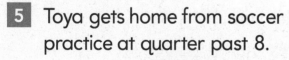 **Use Repeated Reasoning** Draw the clock
hands to show the time.

5 Toya gets home from soccer
practice at quarter past 8.

6 Kelsey plays chess at half
past 4.

Test Prep

What time is shown on the clock? Choose the two correct answers.

7

- ○ quarter past 5
- ○ 30 minutes after 5

- ○ half past 5
- ○ 6 minutes after 5

8

- ○ 15 minutes after 12
- ○ quarter past 12

- ○ half past 12
- ○ 3 minutes after 12

Spiral Review

Make a ten to find the sum. Write the sum.

9 8 + 5 = _____

10 9 + 7 = _____

10 + _____ = _____   10 + _____ = _____

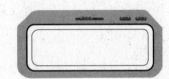

Tell and Write Time with A.M. and P.M.

(MP) Use Tools Write the time. Then circle **a.m.** or **p.m.**

1 get on the bus to go to school

  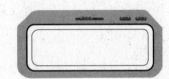

a.m.

p.m.

2 go to the park

  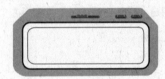

a.m.

p.m.

3 The clock shows the time the sun is high in the sky in the daytime. Write the time. Then circle **noon** or **midnight**.

_____ : _____

noon

midnight

Test Prep

4 What time is shown on the clock? Choose the two correct answers.

- ○ noon
- ○ 12:00
- ○ 1:00
- ○ 12:60

---

5 The clock shows the time Taj practices piano. Write the time. Then circle **a.m.** or **p.m.**

  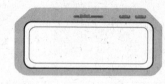

a.m.

p.m.

Spiral Review

6 Write the time in different ways.

_____ : _____

_____ past _____

_____ minutes after _____

Name _____

LESSON 10.1
**More Practice/
Homework**

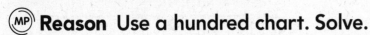

ONLINE
Video Tutorials and
Interactive Examples

Use a Hundred Chart

(MP) **Reason** Use a hundred chart. Solve.

1 Sophia has 45 pennies.
She gives 12 pennies to Brad.
How many pennies does
Sophia have now?

1	2	3	4	5	6	7	8	9	10
11	12	13	14	15	16	17	18	19	20
21	22	23	24	25	26	27	28	29	30
31	32	33	34	35	36	37	38	39	40
41	42	43	44	45	46	47	48	49	50
51	52	53	54	55	56	57	58	59	60
61	62	63	64	65	66	67	68	69	70
71	72	73	74	75	76	77	78	79	80
81	82	83	84	85	86	87	88	89	90
91	92	93	94	95	96	97	98	99	100

_____ pennies

2 Mario has 66 marbles. Tina
gives him 32 more marbles.
How many marbles does
Mario have now?

_____ marbles

3 $74 - 42 =$ _____

4 $95 - 35 =$ _____

5 $85 + 15 =$ _____

6 $25 + 23 =$ _____

Test Prep

Use a hundred chart. Solve.

7 Monique has 62 stars. She earns 34 more stars. How many stars does Monique have now?

1	2	3	4	5	6	7	8	9	10
11	12	13	14	15	16	17	18	19	20
21	22	23	24	25	26	27	28	29	30
31	32	33	34	35	36	37	38	39	40
41	42	43	44	45	46	47	48	49	50
51	52	53	54	55	56	57	58	59	60
61	62	63	64	65	66	67	68	69	70
71	72	73	74	75	76	77	78	79	80
81	82	83	84	85	86	87	88	89	90
91	92	93	94	95	96	97	98	99	100

_____ stars

8 $82 - 24 =$ _____

Spiral Review

9 Write the time in different ways.

_____ : _____

_____ past _____

_____ minutes after _____

10 Draw the clock hands to show the time. Write the time.

quarter past 6

Name _____

LESSON 10.2
**More Practice/
Homework**

ONLINE
Video Tutorials and
Interactive Examples

Use a Number Line

(MP) **Model with Mathematics** Use a number
line. Solve.

1 Isaac has 45 erasers. He gives 12 erasers to Mika.
How many erasers does Isaac have now?

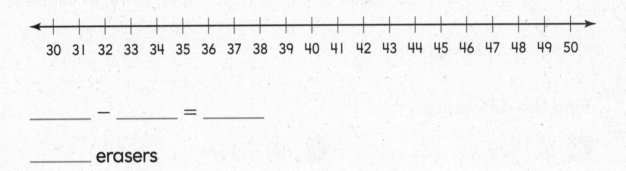

_____ − _____ = _____

_____ erasers

2 Dan sees 15 birds on the way into a park. He sees
another 12 birds on the way out. How many birds
does Dan see?

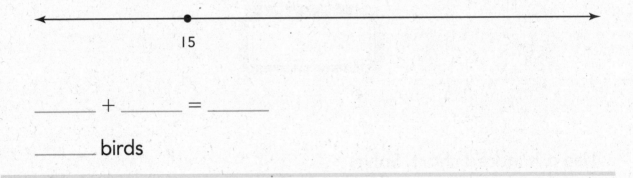

15

_____ + _____ = _____

_____ birds

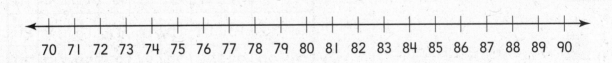

3 75 + 13 = _____   **4** 84 − 14 = _____

Test Prep

Use a number line. Solve.

5 Sasha has 62 stickers. She earns 14 more stickers.
How many stickers does she have?

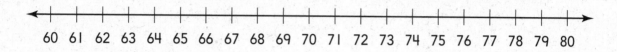

_____ stickers

Find the difference.

6 $67 - 29 =$ _____

7 $54 - 18 =$ _____

Spiral Review

8 Lea wakes up at 25 minutes after 7. Draw the clock
hands to show the time. Write the time.

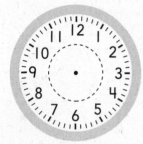 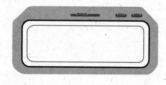

Use a hundred chart. Solve.

9 $16 + 24 =$ _____

10 $31 - 19 =$ _____

11 $47 - 22 =$ _____

1	2	3	4	5	6	7	8	9	10
11	12	13	14	15	16	17	18	19	20
21	22	23	24	25	26	27	28	29	30
31	32	33	34	35	36	37	38	39	40
41	42	43	44	45	46	47	48	49	50

LESSON 10.3
**More Practice/
Homework**

ONLINE
Video Tutorials and
Interactive Examples

Practice Counting Strategies

1 (MP) **Use Tools** Newton sees 37 people go into a store. Then he sees 14 people leave. How many people are still in the store? Solve. Show your work.

1	2	3	4	5	6	7	8	9	10
11	12	13	14	15	16	17	18	19	20
21	22	23	24	25	26	27	28	29	30
31	32	33	34	35	36	37	38	39	40
41	42	43	44	45	46	47	48	49	50

_____ − _____ = _____   _____ people

2 Dory counts flowers while hiking. She counts 21 flowers on the first trail. She counts 19 flowers on the second trail. How many flowers does Dory count?

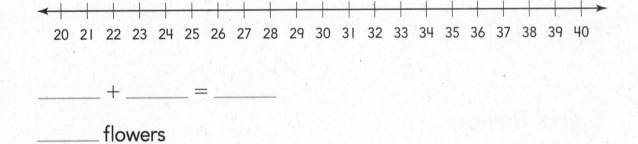

_____ + _____ = _____

_____ flowers

3 (MP) **Attend to Precision** Jamie has 24 stamps in her collection. She buys 15 more stamps. How many stamps does Jamie have now?

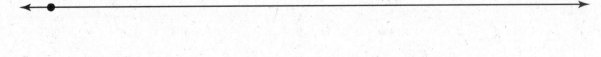

_____ + _____ = _____   _____ stamps

Test Prep

4 Royce lines up 54 markers on the table. He puts 19 markers away. How many markers are still on the table? Fill in the bubble next to the correct answer.

1	2	3	4	5	6	7	8	9	10
11	12	13	14	15	16	17	18	19	20
21	22	23	24	25	26	27	28	29	30
31	32	33	34	35	36	37	38	39	40
41	42	43	44	45	46	47	48	49	50
51	52	53	54	55	56	57	58	59	60
61	62	63	64	65	66	67	68	69	70
71	72	73	74	75	76	77	78	79	80
81	82	83	84	85	86	87	88	89	90
91	92	93	94	95	96	97	98	99	100

○ 73

○ 35

○ 30

Solve.

5 $72 + 24 =$ _____

6 $91 - 43 =$ _____

Spiral Review

Use a number line. Solve.

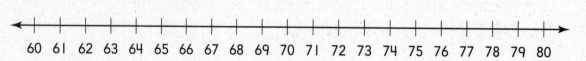

60 61 62 63 64 65 66 67 68 69 70 71 72 73 74 75 76 77 78 79 80

7 $76 - 12 =$ _____

Name _____

LESSON 11.1
**More Practice/
Homework**

ⒺⒹ **ONLINE**
Video Tutorials and
Interactive Examples

Decompose Ones to Add

1 ⓂⓅ **Attend to Precision** Daniel has 17 stickers.
He gets 6 more stickers. How many stickers does
he have now? Draw to show the problem. Make a
new group of ten. Complete each equation to solve.

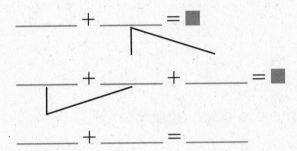

_____ + _____ = ▪

_____ + _____ + _____ = ▪

_____ + _____ = _____

Daniel has _____ stickers now.

---

2 Bruce sees 29 oak trees and 4 maple trees
at the park. How many trees does Bruce see?

_____ trees

---

3 ⓂⓅ **Model with Mathematics** Circle to show
how you make a new group of ten. Complete each
equation to solve.

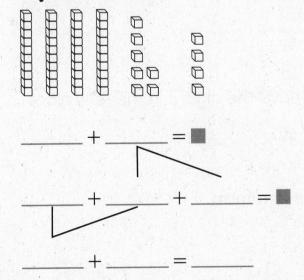

_____ + _____ = ▪

_____ + _____ + _____ = ▪

_____ + _____ = _____

© Houghton Mifflin Harcourt Publishing Company

Test Prep

How can you make a new group of ten?

4 Tristan sees 27 yellow flowers in a garden. He also sees 9 red flowers. How many flowers does Tristan see? Fill in the bubble next to the correct answer.

    ○ 30 + 9   ○ 30 + 6   ○ 27 + 9

5 Make a new group of ten. Complete each equation to solve.

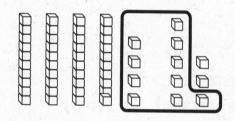

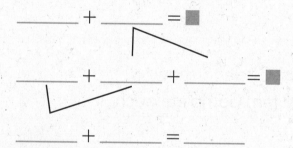

_____ + _____ = ■

_____ + _____ + _____ = ■

_____ + _____ = _____

Spiral Review

6 Circle all of the numbers that have the digit 3 in the tens place.

    236   364   563   346   634

7 Write the number 673 in expanded form.

_____ + _____ + _____

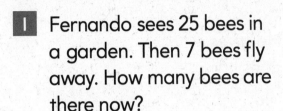
Decompose Ones to Subtract

(MP) Model with Mathematics Break apart ones to subtract. Complete the equations to solve.

1 Fernando sees 25 bees in a garden. Then 7 bees fly away. How many bees are there now?

There are _____ bees now.

2 Mr. Rosario grew 52 pumpkins in his garden. He sold 7 pumpkins. How many pumpkins does he have now?

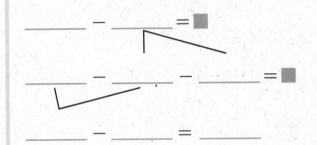

Mr. Rosario has _____ pumpkins now.

3 $17 - 9 =$ ■

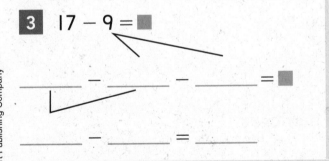

4 $13 - 7 =$ ■

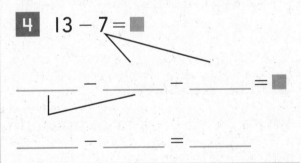

5 **Open Ended** Choose two numbers to subtract. Complete the equations.

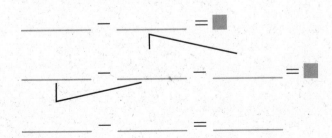

Test Prep

Which equation shows how to break apart the ones to subtract? Fill in the bubble next to the correct answer.

6 Mr. Samuels has 12 yellow flowers. He gives 3 flowers away. How many flowers does Mr. Samuels have now?

- ○ $12 - 3 = \blacksquare$
- ○ $12 - 2 - 3 = \blacksquare$
- ○ $12 - 2 - 1 = \blacksquare$

7 $13 - 8 = \blacksquare$

- ○ $13 - 3 - 5 = \blacksquare$
- ○ $13 - 5 = \blacksquare$
- ○ $13 - 4 - 4 = \blacksquare$

Spiral Review

Write >, <, or = to compare the numbers.

8 349 $\bigcirc$ 493

9 562 $\bigcirc$ 562

10 798 $\bigcirc$ 789

11 445 $\bigcirc$ 454

Name _____

Decompose Numbers to Add

1 (MP) **Model with Mathematics** Matthew has
27 crayons. He has 15 colored pencils. How many
drawing tools does Matthew have? Draw to show
how to make one addend the next tens number.
Complete each equation to solve the problem.

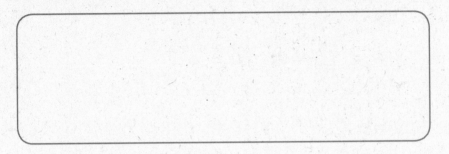

_____ + _____ = ▪

_____ + _____ + _____ = ▪

_____ + _____ = _____

Matthew has _____ drawing tools.

(MP) **Use Structure** Make one addend the next
tens number. Complete each equation to solve.

2 49 + 32 = ▪

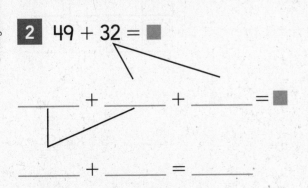

_____ + _____ + _____ = ▪

_____ + _____ = _____

3 27 + 16 = ▪

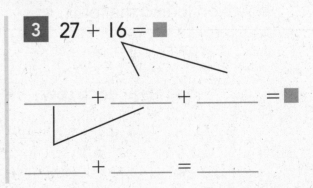

_____ + _____ + _____ = ▪

_____ + _____ = _____

Test Prep

Make one addend the next tens number.
Complete each equation to solve.

4 Aliyah has 28 red beads and 14 yellow beads.
How many beads does she have?

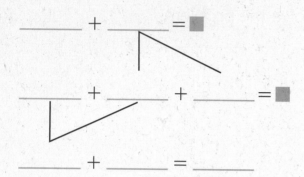

_____ + _____ = ■

_____ + _____ + _____ = ■

_____ + _____ = _____

Aliyah has _____ beads.

5 39 + 12 = ■

_____ + _____ + _____ = ■

_____ + _____ = _____

6 17 + 15 = ■

_____ + _____ + _____ = ■

_____ + _____ = _____

Spiral Review

7 Find the number of rows and the number of squares in each row. Then write an addition equation to find the total.

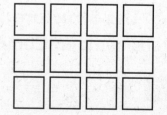

_____ rows

_____ squares in each row

_____ + _____ + _____ = _____

_____ squares

© Houghton Mifflin Harcourt Publishing Company

Decompose Addends as Tens and Ones

(MP) **Model with Mathematics** Break apart the addends into tens and ones. Find the sum.

1 Sam has 32 toy dinosaurs. Greg has 27 toy dinosaurs. How many toy dinosaurs do they have?

   32 $\longrightarrow$ _____ + _____

   + 27 $\longrightarrow$ _____ + _____

   _____ + _____ = _____

   Sam and Greg have _____ toy dinosaurs.

2 18 $\longrightarrow$ _____ + _____

   + 52 $\longrightarrow$ _____ + _____

   _____ + _____ = _____

3 67 $\longrightarrow$ _____ + _____

   + 26 $\longrightarrow$ _____ + _____

   _____ + _____ = _____

4 **Math on the Spot** Julie reads 16 pages of her book in the morning. She reads the same number of pages in the afternoon. How many pages does she read?

_____ pages

Test Prep

5 How can you break apart the addends into tens and ones to find the sum of 37 + 21? Fill in the bubble next to the correct answer.

○ 70 + 3 + 10 + 2

○ 30 + 7 + 20 + 1

○ 3 + 7 + 2 + 1

6 Brian has 34 heart stamps and 33 smiley face stamps. How many stamps does he have?

Brian has _____ stamps.

Spiral Review

7 Look at the clock hands. Write the time.

 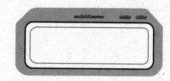

8 Carlos is saving his money. How much money does he have? Count on to solve.

_____, _____, _____

Carlos has _____.

Decompose Numbers to Subtract

1 (MP) **Attend to Precision** Mrs. Danza has 46 flowers. She gives 24 flowers to a friend. How many flowers does Mrs. Danza have now? Break apart the number being subtracted into tens and ones. Subtract the tens, then subtract the ones. Find the difference.

_____ − _____ = ■

_____ − _____ = _____

_____ − _____ = _____

Mrs. Danza has _____ flowers now.

2 **Math on the Spot** Jane has 45 toys in a box. She takes some toys out. Now there are 22 toys in the box. How many toys does Jane take out of the box?

_____ toys

3 **Open Ended** Choose two numbers to subtract. Complete the equations.

_____ − _____ = ■

_____ − _____ = _____

_____ − _____ = _____

Test Prep

4 Which shows a way to break apart 18?
Fill in the bubble next to the correct answer.

○ 1 + 8   ○ 10 + 8   ○ 18 + 10

5 Sandra has 29 marbles. 13 marbles are green.
The rest are blue. How many blue marbles does
Sandra have? Break apart and subtract to solve.

_____ − _____ = ■

_____ − _____ = _____

_____ − _____ = _____

Cassandra has _____ blue marbles.

Spiral Review

6

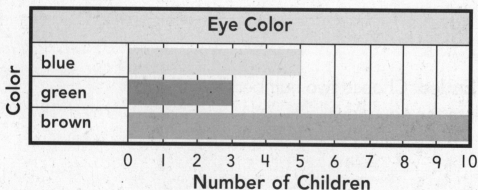

Use the bar graph to solve the problem.

How many more children have
brown eyes than have blue eyes?   _____ more children

© Houghton Mifflin Harcourt Publishing Company

LESSON 12.1
**More Practice/
Homework**

ONLINE
Video Tutorials and
Interactive Examples

Represent Regrouping for Addition

**Use tools or draw to solve. Regroup if you
need to.**

1 (MP) **Reason** Mr. Cruz has 53 nails. Ms. Cruz
has 38 nails. How many nails do they have?

_____ nails

Explain why you can regroup to solve this problem.

_____

_____

_____

2 (MP) **Use Structure** On Tuesday, Lucky Farms takes
48 cartons of milk to a bakery. They also take
39 cartons of milk to a grocery store. How many
cartons of milk does Lucky Farms take on Tuesday?

_____ cartons of milk

3 (MP) **Use Tools** Add 28 and 47. Write how many tens
and ones. Write the sum.

Tens	Ones

_____ tens _____ ones

_____

Test Prep

4 There are 54 bees inside a hive. There are 26 bees outside the hive. How many bees are there?

Tens	Ones

_____ bees

---

5 For which problem do you need to regroup 10 ones as 1 ten? Fill in the bubble next to the correct answer.

○ Add 17 to 32.

○ Add 24 to 59.

○ Add 43 and 35.

Spiral Review

6 Ben has 15 stuffed animals. He puts 8 of the stuffed animals in his toy box. The rest are on a shelf. How many stuffed animals are on the shelf?

_____ stuffed animals

LESSON 12.2
**More Practice/
Homework**

◎Ed **ONLINE**
Video Tutorials and
Interactive Examples

Represent Regrouping
for Subtraction

Use tools or draw to solve. Regroup if you need to.

1 **(MP) Attend to Precision** There are 24 fish
in a pond. Then 16 fish swim away.
How many fish are there now?

Tens	Ones

_____ fish

Do you need to regroup? Explain.

_____

_____

2 **Math on the Spot** Billy has 18 fewer
marbles than Sara. Sara has 34 marbles.
How many marbles does Billy have?

Tens	Ones

_____ marbles

3 **(MP) Use Tools** Subtract 19 from 51.
Write the difference.

Tens	Ones

_____

Test Prep

4 There are 92 children playing baseball. There are 78 children playing soccer. How many more children are playing baseball than soccer?

Tens	Ones

_____ more children

5 For which problem do you need to regroup 1 ten as 10 ones? Fill in the bubble next to the correct answer.

○ Subtract 16 from 38.

○ Subtract 27 from 85.

○ Subtract 51 from 72.

Spiral Review

6 At a park, there are 11 places to sit. There are 6 picnic tables. The rest are benches. How many benches are there? Write a subtraction fact and a related addition fact for the problem. Then solve.

_____ − _____ = _____

_____ + _____ = _____

_____ benches

Represent and Record Two-Digit Addition

1 (MP) **Use Structure** Bob finds 17 shells on the beach. Kayla finds 24 shells on the beach. How many shells do they find?

_____ shells

Do you need to regroup 10 ones as 1 ten?

_____

Explain. _____

_____

Tens	Ones
☐	
1	7
+ 2	4

2 **Math on the Spot** Tim has 27 stickers. Margo has 48 stickers. How many more stickers would they need to have 100 stickers altogether?

_____ more stickers

3 (MP) **Use Tools** Add 84 and 5.

Tens	Ones
☐	
8	4
+	5

Tens	Ones

Test Prep

4 Joe draws 18 flowers on his paper. Then he draws 24 more flowers. How many flowers does Joe draw? Fill in the bubble next to the correct answer.

Tens	Ones
□	
1	8
+ 2	4

○ 14

○ 42

○ 44

5 There are 57 cars and 28 trucks in a parking lot. How many cars and trucks are in the parking lot?

Tens	Ones
□	
5	7
+ 2	8

_____ cars and trucks

6 For which problem will you need to regroup? Fill in the bubble next to the correct answer.

○ 36 + 41   ○ 33 + 27   ○ 34 + 5

Spiral Review

7 Look at the clock hands. Write the time.

LESSON 12.4
**More Practice/
Homework**

Ed **ONLINE**
Video Tutorials and
Interactive Examples

Represent and Record
Two-Digit Subtraction

1 (MP) **Use Structure** There are 36 boats in
the bay. Then 14 boats sail away. How
many boats are there now?

_____ boats

Did you regroup 10 ones as 1 ten? _____

Explain. _____

_____

Tens	Ones
☐	☐
3	6
− 1	4

2 (MP) **Attend to Precision** Mr. Daniels has
42 tennis balls. He hits 24 of them over a wall.
How many tennis balls does Mr. Daniels
have now?

_____ tennis balls

Tens	Ones
☐	☐
4	2
− 2	4

3 **Math on the Spot** Claire's puzzle has 94 pieces.
She has used 38 pieces so far. How many puzzle
pieces have not been used yet?

_____ puzzle pieces

4 (MP) **Use Tools** Subtract 9 from 76.

Tens	Ones
☐	☐
7	6
−	9

Tens	Ones

Test Prep

5 There are 37 children on a bus. Then 18 children get off the bus. How many children are on the bus now? Fill in the bubble next to the correct answer.

Tens	Ones
□	□
3	7
− 1	8

○ 19

○ 21

○ 55

6 Mrs. Carter buys 30 tomatoes. She uses 18 tomatoes to make soup. How many tomatoes does Mrs. Carter have now?

_____ tomatoes

7 For which problem will you need to regroup 1 ten as 10 ones? Fill in the bubble next to the correct answer.

○ 87 − 43

○ 89 − 9

○ 82 − 64

Spiral Review

8 What is the total value of the bills shown?

_____

LESSON 12.5
**More Practice/
Homework**

ONLINE
Ed Video Tutorials and
Interactive Examples

Add Two-Digit Numbers

1 **(MP) Attend to Precision** There are
29 children in a classroom. Then 3 more
children walk in. How many children
are in the classroom now?

Tens	Ones
2	9
+	3

_____ children

---

2 **(MP) Reason** There are 14 basketball
games played in the morning. There are
15 basketball games played at night.
How many games are played?

1	4
+ 1	5

_____ games

Do you need to regroup 10 ones as 1 ten? Explain.

_____

_____

_____

---

3 **Math on the Spot** Jin has 22 books about cats
and 38 books about dogs. He gives 5 books to his
sister. How many books does Jin have now?

_____ books

Test Prep

Fill in the bubble next to the correct answer.

4 There are 18 computers in the store. Then 14 more computers are put in the store. How many computers are in the store now?

○ 4 computers

○ 32 computers

○ 42 computers

5 Kalil jumps rope for 17 minutes before school. He jumps rope for 18 minutes after school. How many minutes does Kalil jump rope?

○ 25 minutes   ○ 35 minutes   ○ 45 minutes

6 Add. Regroup if you need to.

$$\begin{array}{r} 3\ \ 6 \\ +\ 5\ \ 4 \\ \hline \end{array}$$

Spiral Review

7 There are 3 rows of trees at a fruit farm. There are 5 trees in each row. How many trees are there? Draw the trees. Write an addition equation to solve the problem.

_____ + _____ + _____ = _____

_____ trees

LESSON 12.6
**More Practice/
Homework**

ONLINE
Video Tutorials and
Interactive Examples

Subtract Two-Digit Numbers

Solve. Regroup if you need to.

1 (MP) **Attend to Precision** In gym class, 51 children
vote to play kickball. 27 children vote to play
soccer. How many more children vote for
kickball than soccer?

Tens	Ones
□	□
5	1
− 2	7

_____ more children

2 There are 36 snails in Mrs. King's garden.
Then 17 snails crawl away. How many
snails are there now?

_____ snails

Do you need to regroup 1 ten as 10 ones? Explain.

_____

_____

_____

3 (MP) **Use Repeated Reasoning** Katie writes a story
for 26 minutes. Spencer writes a story for 19 minutes.
For how many fewer minutes does Spencer write?

_____ fewer minutes

Test Prep

Fill in the bubble next to the correct answer.

4 Mrs. Bailey has 75 tokens. She gives Stephanie 47 tokens. How many tokens does Mrs. Bailey have now?

  ○ 38 tokens   ○ 32 tokens   ○ 28 tokens

5 Sheng has 22 pencils. His sister has 13 pencils. How many fewer pencils does Sheng's sister have than Sheng?

  ○ 9 fewer pencils

  ○ 11 fewer pencils

  ○ 35 fewer pencils

6 Subtract. Regroup if you need to.

$$\begin{array}{r} 7\;\;0 \\ -\;2\;\;6 \\ \hline \end{array}$$

Spiral Review

7 There are 365 pennies in a jar. What is the value of the digit 3?

_____ hundreds or _____

Rewrite Addition Problems

(MP) **Attend to Precision** Rewrite the addition. Find the sum.

1 There are 39 red apples in a basket. There are 13 green apples in another basket. How many apples are there?

$39 + 13 = \blacksquare$

+

_____ apples

2 $27 + 16 = \blacksquare$

+

3 $57 + 33 = \blacksquare$

+

4 **Math on the Spot** For which of these problems could you find the sum without rewriting it? Explain.

$27 + 54$ $34 + 30$ $26 + 17$ $48 + 38$

_____

_____

_____

Test Prep

5 How can you rewrite 45 + 12? Fill in the bubble next to the correct answer.

○
$$
\begin{array}{c|c}
4 & 5 \\
+ 1 & 2 \\
\end{array}
$$

○
$$
\begin{array}{c|c}
4 & 5 \\
+ 2 & 1 \\
\end{array}
$$

○
$$
\begin{array}{c|c}
5 & 4 \\
+ 1 & 2 \\
\end{array}
$$

6 Lane has 56 paper clips. He gets 25 more paper clips. How many paper clips does Lane have now? Find the sum.

56 + 25 = ■

_____ paper clips

Spiral Review

Look at the clock hands. Write the time.

7

8

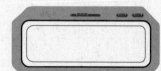

ONLINE
Video Tutorials and
Interactive Examples

Rewrite Subtraction Problems

(MP) **Attend to Precision** Rewrite the subtraction. Find the difference.

1 Stephanie has 61 beads on her necklace. Then 29 of the beads fall off. How many beads does Stephanie have on her necklace now?

$61 - 29 = \blacksquare$

_____ beads

2 $60 - 45 = \blacksquare$

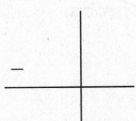

3 $82 - 39 = \blacksquare$

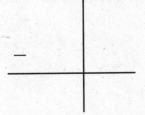

4 **Math on the Spot** For which of these problems could you find the difference without rewriting it? Explain.

$35 - 9$ $78 - 10$ $54 - 38$ $92 - 39$

_____

_____

_____

Test Prep

5 How can you rewrite 63 − 15? Fill in the bubble next to the correct answer.

○
$$\begin{array}{c|c} 6 & 5 \\ -1 & 3 \end{array}$$

○
$$\begin{array}{c|c} 6 & 3 \\ -1 & 5 \end{array}$$

○
$$\begin{array}{c|c} 5 & 1 \\ -3 & 6 \end{array}$$

6 A teacher has 47 pencils. He gives 18 pencils to the students. How many pencils does he have now? Find the difference.

47 − 18 = ■　　　　　　　　　　＿＿＿ pencils

Spiral Review

Count on to find the total value of each group of coins.

7

＿＿＿ ¢, ＿＿＿ ¢, ＿＿＿ ¢

8

＿＿＿ ¢, ＿＿＿ ¢, ＿＿＿ ¢, ＿＿＿ ¢, ＿＿＿ ¢

9

＿＿＿ ¢, ＿＿＿ ¢, ＿＿＿ ¢, ＿＿＿ ¢

Use Addition and a Number Line to Subtract

Use the number line. Count up to find the difference.

1 (MP) **Use Tools** There are 64 crackers in a box. Some children eat 59 of the crackers. How many crackers are there now?

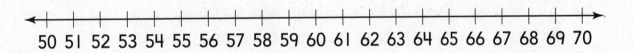

50 51 52 53 54 55 56 57 58 59 60 61 62 63 64 65 66 67 68 69 70

There are _____ crackers now.

2 **Math on the Spot** There are 55 books on the table. Sandra picks up some of the books. Now there are 49 books on the table. How many books does Sandra pick up?

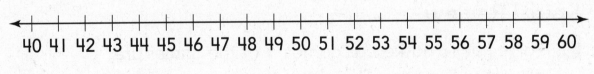

40 41 42 43 44 45 46 47 48 49 50 51 52 53 54 55 56 57 58 59 60

55 − _____ = 49

_____ books

3 56 − 48 = _____

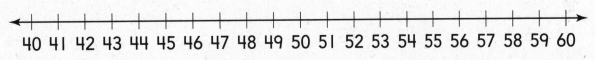

40 41 42 43 44 45 46 47 48 49 50 51 52 53 54 55 56 57 58 59 60

Test Prep

4 There are 43 mystery books at the library. 34 of the mystery books are checked out. How many mystery books are at the library now?

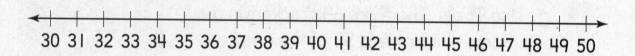

There are _____ mystery books at the library now.

5 Mr. Sanders buys 32 lemons. He uses some lemons to make lemonade. Now he has 26 lemons. How many lemons does Mr. Sanders use to make lemonade? Fill in the bubble next to the correct answer.

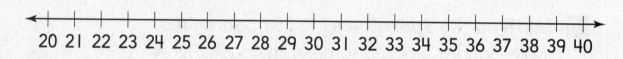

○ 8   ○ 6   ○ 4

Spiral Review

6 Paige has 16 basketball games. 7 of the games are played on Saturday. The rest of the games are played on Sunday. How many games are played on Sunday? Find the difference. Show the tens fact you used.

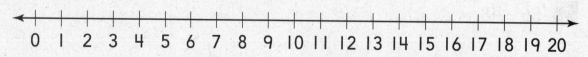

16 − _____ = 10   10 − _____ = _____   _____ games

Name _____

LESSON 13.4
**More Practice/
Homework**

ONLINE
Video Tutorials and
Interactive Examples

Add 3 Two-Digit Numbers Using Strategies and Properties

Solve. Show your work.

1 (MP) **Reason** Nia has 13 red pens, 24 purple pens, and 18 blue pens. How many pens does she have?

```
  1 | 3
  2 | 4
+ 1 | 8
------
```

_____ pens

---

2 **Math on the Spot** Sophia has 34 marbles. She buys 17 more marbles. Then John gives her 43 marbles. How many marbles does Sophia have now?

```
  3 | 4
  1 | 7
+ 4 | 3
------
```

_____ marbles

(MP) **Use Structure** Find the sum.

3
```
  2 | 4
  2 | 5
+ 2 | 1
------
```

4
```
  2 | 4
  2 | 2
+ 4 | 8
------
```

5
```
  5 | 2
  2 | 8
+ 1 | 1
------
```

6
```
  1 | 5
  4 | 9
+ 3 | 3
------
```

Test Prep

7 Sean uses 24 blue blocks, 38 red blocks, and 17 green blocks to make a castle. How many blocks does Sean use?

```
  2 │ 4
  3 │ 8
+ 1 │ 7
────┼────
```

_____ blocks

8 There are 48 turkey sandwiches, 29 salads, and 21 baked potatoes in the lunchroom. How many food items are in the lunchroom? Fill in the bubble next to the correct answer.

```
  4 │ 8
  2 │ 9
+ 2 │ 1
────┼────
```

○ 87

○ 90

○ 98

Spiral Review

Write the number in expanded form.

9 564 _____ + _____ + _____

10 791 _____ + _____ + _____

11 832 _____ + _____ + _____

LESSON 13.5
**More Practice/
Homework**

 **ONLINE**
Video Tutorials and
Interactive Examples

Add 4 Two-Digit Numbers Using Strategies and Properties

1 Paul counts 23 pumpkins. Kayla counts
18 pumpkins. Fran counts 22 pumpkins.
Ned counts 11 pumpkins. How many
pumpkins do they count? Find the sum.
Show your work.

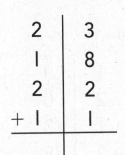

```
  2 | 3
  1 | 8
  2 | 2
+ 1 | 1
----+----
```

_____ pumpkins

---

2 **Math on the Spot** Laney adds four numbers that
have a total of 146. She spills some juice over one
number. What is that number?

```
  2 | 4
  4 | 7
+ 3 | 0
----+----
```

```
  1 | 4 | 6
- _ | _ | _
----+---+----
```

$24 + 47 + \blacksquare + 30 = 146$

$146 - \underline{\hphantom{000}} = \underline{\hphantom{000}}$

(MP) **Attend to Precision** Find the sum. Show your work.

3
```
  1 | 6
  2 | 3
  3 | 8
+ 1 | 0
----+----
```

4
```
  2 | 5
  2 | 2
  2 | 5
+ 1 | 7
----+----
```

5
```
  2 | 0
  4 | 8
  1 | 3
+ 1 | 7
----+----
```

Test Prep

6 There are 10 blue balloons, 13 red balloons, 24 green balloons, and 30 yellow balloons in a store. How many balloons are there? Find the sum.

```
  1   0
  1   3
  2   4
+ 3   0
```

_____ balloons

7 Zella counts the birds she sees. She sees 14 blue birds, 20 red birds, 13 black birds, and 28 yellow birds. How many birds does Zella see? Fill in the bubble next to the correct answer.

```
  1   4
  2   0
  1   3
+ 2   8
```

○ 55   ○ 62   ○ 75

Spiral Review

Rewrite the addition. Find the sum.

8 $44 + 38 = \blacksquare$

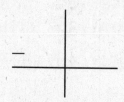

9 $\blacksquare = 56 + 26$

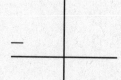

Rewrite the subtraction. Find the difference.

10 $54 - 26 = \blacksquare$

11 $77 - 38 = \blacksquare$

Use Drawings to Represent
Addition and Subtraction Situations

Complete the bar model and the equation. Solve.

1 ⓂⓅ **Use Structure** Matthew finds 9 red leaves. Greg
finds 6 yellow leaves. How many leaves do they find?

_____

_____ + _____ = _____

_____ leaves

2 **Math on the Spot** Anne has 16 blue clips and
9 red clips. How many more blue clips than red
clips does she have?

_____

_____ − _____ = _____

_____ more blue clips

3 The American flag has 13 stripes. There are 7 red stripes
and the rest are white. How many of the stripes are white?

_____

_____ − _____ = _____

_____ stripes

Test Prep

4 Which equation matches the bar model? Fill in the bubble next to the correct answer.

5	9

14

○ $14 + 5 = 19$

○ $9 + 5 = 14$

○ $9 - 5 = 4$

---

5 Gia has 20 apples. She gives away 5 apples.
How many apples does Gia have now?
Fill in the bubble next to the correct answer.

$20 - 5 = $ _____

○ 20

○ 15

○ 5

Spiral Review

Find the sum. Show your work.

6
```
  5 2
  2 6
    8
+ 2 1
_____
```

7
```
  3 0
  1 2
+   3
_____
```

© Houghton Mifflin Harcourt Publishing Company

Use Equations to Represent Addition and Subtraction Situations

(MP) **Use Structure** Complete the bar model. Write an equation with a ■ for the unknown number. Write and solve your equation.

1 Lara plays tennis for 7 minutes. Mari plays tennis for 4 more minutes than Lara. How many minutes does Mari play tennis?

_____

_____

_____ minutes

2 Pao makes 15 cards. Marcus makes 9 fewer cards than Pao. How many cards does Marcus make?

_____

_____

_____ cards

3 **Math on the Spot** There are some ducks in a pond. 4 more ducks join them. Now there are 13 ducks in the pond. How many ducks were in the pond to start?

_____

_____

_____ ducks

Test Prep

4 Ian has 9 red pencils and some blue pencils. He has 17 pencils in all. How many blue pencils does Ian have? Write an equation with a ■ for the unknown number. Solve.

_____   _____ blue pencils

5 There are 19 people at the bus stop. 12 people sit on benches. How many people do not sit? Which bar model represents the problem? Fill in the bubble next to the correct answer.

○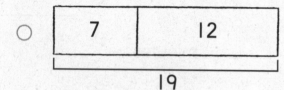

○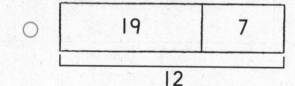

○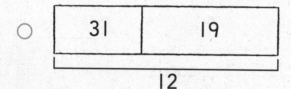

Spiral Review

Find the sum. Show your work.

6
```
    2   2
    1   6
        9
+   2   1
_____
```

7
```
    2   3
    2   4
    1   0
+   3   8
_____
```

LESSON 14.3
**More Practice/
Homework**

ONLINE
Video Tutorials and
Interactive Examples

Use Drawings and Equations to Represent Two-Digit Addition

1 (MP) **Model with Mathematics** Nate has
23 blocks. Doris has 31 more blocks than Nate.
How many blocks does Doris have? Complete
the bar model. Write an addition equation
with a ■ for the unknown number.
Write and solve your equation.

_____

_____

_____ blocks

2 **Math on the Spot** There are three groups of
owls. There are 16 owls in each of the first two
groups. There are 54 owls in all. How many owls
are in the third group?

16	16

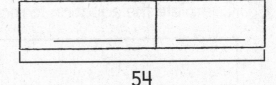

54

_____

_____

_____

_____ owls

Test Prep

3 Ayana counts some flowers. Then she counts 20 more flowers. She counts 39 flowers in all. How many flowers did Ayana count to start? Fill in the bubble next to the correct answer.

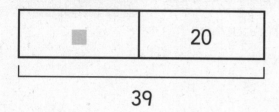

○ 19   ○ 20   ○ 39

4 Haven has 5 more stickers than Noel. Noel has 12 stickers. Which equation represents how many stickers Haven has? Fill in the bubble next to the correct answer.

○ ■ + 5 = 12

○ 12 + 5 = ■

○ 12 − ■ = 5

Spiral Review

5 Complete the equation to match the bar model.

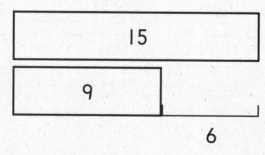

_____ − _____ = _____

Name _____

LESSON 14.4
More Practice/ Homework

ONLINE
Video Tutorials and
Interactive Examples

Use Drawings and Equations to Represent Two-Digit Subtraction

1 (MP) **Use Structure** There are 45 birds in a field. 16 of the birds fly away. How many birds are in the field now? Complete the bar model. Write a subtraction equation with a ■ for the unknown number. Write and solve your equation.

_____ birds

2 **Math on the Spot** Jennifer writes 8 poems at school and 13 poems at home. She writes 5 more poems than Nell. How many poems does Nell write? Complete each bar model and write equations to solve.

8	13

J _____

N _____

5

_____ poems

Test Prep

3 Which equation matches the bar model? Fill in the bubble next to the correct answer.

39

17
22

○ $17 + 39 = 56$

○ $39 - 17 = 22$

○ $22 - 17 = 5$

---

4 Lou has 57 berries. Ari has 23 fewer berries than Lou. How many berries does Ari have? Complete the bar model. Write an addition equation with a ■ for the unknown number. Write and solve your equation.

57

_____

_____

_____

_____ berries

Spiral Review

Write an equation to represent the problem. Use a ■ for the unknown number. Write and solve your equation.

5 There are 40 cars in a parking lot. 17 cars are red. How many cars are not red?

_____

_____   _____ cars

LESSON 15.1
**More Practice/
Homework**

ONLINE
Video Tutorials and
Interactive Examples

Solve Addition Word Problems

Write an equation to show the problem. Solve.

1   (MP) **Model with Mathematics** Mr. Clark
takes 59 photos with a camera. He takes
34 fewer photos than Mr. Watts.
How many photos does Mr. Watts take?

_____

_____

Mr. Watts takes _____ photos.

2   There are some frogs on a log. Then 14 frogs hop
onto the log. Now there are 29 frogs on
the log. How many frogs are on the log to start?

_____

_____

There are _____ frogs on the log to start.

3   **Open Ended** Write a word problem for this
equation.

25 + 47 = 72

_____

_____

_____

Test Prep

4 Kay eats 17 strawberries. Stephanie eats 25 blackberries. How many berries do Kay and Stephanie eat?

Which equation shows the problem? Fill in the bubble next to the correct answer.

○ ■ = 25 − 17

○ ■ + 17 = 25

○ ■ = 17 + 25

5 There are some books in a bookcase. Nancy puts 21 more books in the bookcase. Now there are 40 books in the bookcase. How many books are there to start?

Write an equation to show the problem. Solve.

_____

_____

There are _____ books in the bookcase to start.

Spiral Review

Add. Regroup if you need to.

6
```
  4 | 5
+ 1 | 9
```

7
```
  3 | 6
+ 1 | 4
```

8
```
  7 | 2
+ 2 | 4
```

© Houghton Mifflin Harcourt Publishing Company

LESSON 15.2
**More Practice/
Homework**

ONLINE
Video Tutorials and
Interactive Examples

Solve Subtraction Word Problems

Write an equation to show the problem. Solve.

1 Ⓜ️ **Reason** Cody builds a sandcastle with 32 towers. His sandcastle has 13 more towers than Asher's sandcastle. How many towers does Asher's sandcastle have?

_____

_____

Asher's sandcastle has _____ towers.

2 Ⓜ️ **Model with Mathematics** At lunchtime, 32 children drink milk. 58 children drink orange juice. How many more children drink orange juice?

_____

_____

_____ more children drink orange juice.

3 Ⓜ️ **Use Structure** Keisha has a bag of ribbons. She takes 29 ribbons out of the bag. Now there are 17 ribbons in the bag. How many ribbons are in the bag to start?

_____

_____

_____ ribbons are in the bag to start.

Test Prep

4 There are 49 books on a shelf. Bill takes 26 books off the shelf. How many books are on the shelf now? Which equation shows the problem? Fill in the bubble next to the correct answer.

○ $49 + 26 = \blacksquare$

○ $49 - 26 = \blacksquare$

○ $\blacksquare - 26 = 49$

5 Mr. Hall folds 27 shirts. He has 15 more shirts to fold. How many shirts does Mr. Hall have to start?

Write an equation to show the problem. Solve.

_____

_____

Mr. Hall has _____ shirts to start.

Spiral Review

Subtract. Regroup if you need to.

6
$$\begin{array}{r} 4\ \ 6 \\ -\ 2\ \ 9 \\ \hline \end{array}$$

7
$$\begin{array}{r} 3\ \ 8 \\ -\ 2\ \ 4 \\ \hline \end{array}$$

8
$$\begin{array}{r} 8\ \ 2 \\ -\ 3\ \ 5 \\ \hline \end{array}$$

Name _____

Solve Multistep Addition and Subtraction Problems

ONLINE
Video Tutorials and
Interactive Examples

(MP) **Model with Mathematics** Write two equations. Solve.

1 Julia and Mason each pick 9 apples.
They lose 5 apples on the way home.
How many apples do they have now?

_____

_____

Julia and Mason have _____ apples now.

2 There are 17 dogs at a park. 8 are pugs. The
rest are poodles. 3 poodles are black. How many
poodles are not black?

_____

_____

_____ poodles are not black.

3 **Math on the Spot** Shelby has 35 rocks. She finds
36 more rocks at a park and gives 28 rocks to
George. How many rocks does she have now?

 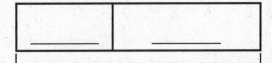

_____   _____

Now Shelby has _____ rocks.

© Houghton Mifflin Harcourt Publishing Company

Test Prep

4 Kathy buys 8 oranges. She gives Jake 3 of the oranges. Then she buys 3 more oranges. How many oranges does Kathy have now?

Fill in the bubble next to the correct answer.

○ 11   ○ 8   ○ 5

5 David has 6 shells. He finds 3 more shells. Then he gives 2 shells to Wendy. How many shells does David have now?

Write two equations. Solve.

_____

_____

David has _____ shells now.

Spiral Review

Choose two addends to add first. Circle the addends. Write the sum.

6 $6 + 4 + 2 =$ _____

7 $7 + 1 + 3 =$ _____

8 $4 + 2 + 4 =$ _____

9 $3 + 5 + 4 =$ _____

LESSON 16.1
**More Practice/
Homework**

ONLINE
Video Tutorials and
Interactive Examples

Using Drawings to Represent Three-Digit Addition

1 (MP) **Attend to Precision** Mr. Fox travels 135 miles on Sunday and 251 miles on Monday. How many miles does Mr. Fox travel? Draw quick pictures. Write the number of hundreds, tens, and ones. Solve.

Hundreds	Tens	Ones

_____ hundreds _____ tens _____ ones   _____ miles

2 **Math on the Spot** Use the quick pictures to find the two numbers being added. Then write how many hundreds, tens, and ones in all. Write the number.

Hundreds	Tens	Ones

Add _____ and _____.

_____ hundreds _____ tens _____ ones

_____

Test Prep

3 Izzy makes a concrete model to add 472 + 325. What is the total number of hundreds, tens, and ones? Fill in the bubble next to the correct answer.

Hundreds	Tens	Ones

○ 4 hundreds, 9 tens, 7 ones

○ 7 hundreds, 9 tens, 7 ones

○ 3 hundreds, 2 tens, 5 ones

Spiral Review

4 Break apart ones to subtract. Complete the equations to solve.

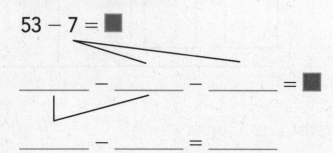

$53 - 7 = \blacksquare$

_____ − _____ − _____ = $\blacksquare$

_____ − _____ = _____

5 What number is 100 more than 481? _____

© Houghton Mifflin Harcourt Publishing Company

LESSON 16.2
**More Practice/
Homework**

 ONLINE
Video Tutorials and
Interactive Examples

Decompose Three-Digit Addends

1 (MP) **Use Structure** The baker sells 165 loaves
of bread on Monday and 132 loaves on Tuesday.
How many loaves does the baker sell on both
days? Break apart addends to solve.

165 ⟶ _____ + _____ + _____

+ 132 ⟶ _____ + _____ + _____

_____   _____   _____

_____ loaves

2 **Math on the Spot** Mr. Jones has 165 sheets
of blue paper, 100 sheets of red paper, and
241 sheets of green paper. How many sheets
of paper does he have?

_____ sheets of paper

3 **Open Ended** A problem has been started for
you below. Choose a second three-digit addend.
Find the sum.

412 ⟶ _____ + _____ + _____

+ _____ ⟶ _____ + _____ + _____

_____ + _____ + _____ = _____

Test Prep

4 Mr. Hall has 130 books in his library. He adds 254 more books to his library. How many books does Mr. Hall have now? Break apart addends to solve.

130 ⟶ _____ + _____ + _____

+ 254 ⟶ _____ + _____ + _____

_____   _____   _____

_____ books

Spiral Review

5 Draw a quick picture for the number 346.

Write how many hundreds, tens, and ones.

_____ hundreds _____ tens _____ ones

6 Explain how to regroup to solve 83 − 28.

_____

_____

_____

LESSON 16.3
**More Practice/
Homework**

 ONLINE
Video Tutorials and
Interactive Examples

Represent Regrouping for Addition

1 (MP) **Reason** There are 256 tall boxes and
171 short boxes at the shipping store.
How many boxes are there altogether?
Add to solve.

Hundreds	Tens	Ones

Hundreds	Tens	Ones
☐ 2	☐ 5	6
+ 1	7	1

_____ boxes

2 **Math on the Spot** Miko wrote
this problem. What are the
missing digits?

☐ ☐ 6

    4 5 ☐
+ _____
    6 9 0

(MP) **Use Structure** Use tools or draw pictures. Find the sum.

3

Hundreds	Tens	Ones
☐ 1	☐ 0	9
+ 3	3	8

4

Hundreds	Tens	Ones
☐ 5	☐ 8	8
+ 1	6	1

one hundred forty-three

Test Prep

5 Mary has 166 green beads and 140 blue beads. How many beads does she have?

Hundreds	Tens	Ones
☐ ☐	‖‖‖‖‖ ‖‖‖‖	○○○○○○○○

	Hundreds	Tens	Ones
	1	6	6
+	1	4	0

_____ beads

Spiral Review

Draw the clock hands to show the time.
Write the time.

6 45 minutes after 9

7 10 minutes after 1

LESSON 16.4
**More Practice/
Homework**

ONLINE
Ed
Video Tutorials and
Interactive Examples

Add Three-Digit Numbers

1 (MP) **Attend to Precision** Rita has 180 bracelets.
She makes 150 more bracelets. How many bracelets
does she have now? Find the sum.

Hundreds	Tens	Ones
☐	☐	
1	8	0
+ 1	5	0

_____ bracelets

2 Write the missing digits.

Hundreds	Tens	Ones
☐	☐	
6		7
+ 2	3	
	6	2

(MP) **Use Structure** Find the sum.

3

Hundreds	Tens	Ones
☐	☐	
6	6	3
+ 2	5	2

4

Hundreds	Tens	Ones
☐	☐	
1	7	1
+ 2	2	9

Test Prep

5 Find the sum. Fill in the bubble next to the correct answer.

387
+ 461

Hundreds	Tens	Ones
3	8	7
+ 4	6	1

○ 738   ○ 838   ○ 848

---

6 At Tim's Pizza Shop, 179 pizzas were sold on Friday and 226 pizzas were sold on Saturday. How many pizzas were sold on Friday and Saturday?

_____ pizzas

Hundreds	Tens	Ones
1	7	9
+ 2	2	6

Spiral Review

7 Mrs. Simi has these bills. How much money does she have?

Mrs. Simi has _____.

Represent Three-Digit Subtraction

Make a concrete model or draw a visual model
to solve.

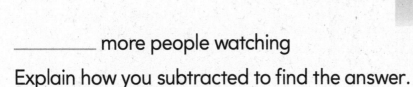

1 **(MP) Reason** There are 457 people running and
988 people watching at a race. How many
more people are watching than running?

_____ more people watching

Explain how you subtracted to find the answer.

_____

_____

2 **Math on the Spot** There are 164 children and
31 adults who see a movie in the morning.
There are 125 children who see the movie in the
afternoon. How many fewer children saw the
movie in the afternoon than in the morning?

_____ fewer children

Draw a visual model to solve.

3 Subtract 412 from 536.

_____

Test Prep

4 Which subtraction problem does this concrete model represent? Fill in the bubble next to the correct answer.

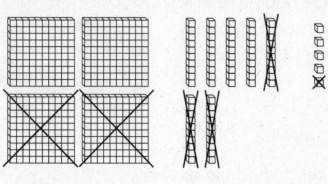

○ 475 – 123 = ■   ○ 475 – 231 = ■   ○ 475 – 213 = ■

---

5 There are 678 fish in a lake. Of those fish, 417 are not catfish. The rest are catfish. How many catfish are in the lake?

678 – 417 = ■

_____ catfish

Spiral Review

Rewrite the addition. Find the sum.

6 35 + 39 = ■

7 63 + 15 = ■

LESSON 17.2
**More Practice/
Homework**

ⓔ Ed ONLINE
Video Tutorials and
Interactive Examples

Represent Regrouping
for Subtraction

1 (MP) **Use Structure** There are 316 birds in trees. Then 162 of the birds fly away. How many birds are still in trees? Write and draw to solve.

Hundreds	Tens	Ones
☐	☐	
3	1	6
− 1	6	2

There are still _____ birds in trees.

---

2 **Math on the Spot** Sam makes two towers. He uses 184 blocks for the first tower. He uses 349 blocks in all. For which tower does he use more blocks?

Hundreds	Tens	Ones
☐	☐	
3	4	9
− 1	8	4

He uses more blocks for

the _____ tower.

Explain how you solved the problem.

_____

_____

_____

Test Prep

3 Which subtraction problem does this concrete model represent? Fill in the bubble next to the correct answer.

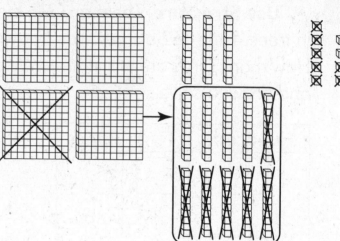

- ○ $339 - 167 = \blacksquare$
- ○ $439 - 167 = \blacksquare$
- ○ $439 - 267 = \blacksquare$

4 Mr. Toby has 546 tickets to sell. He sells 373 tickets. How many tickets does Mr. Toby have left?

Hundreds	Tens	Ones
☐	☐	
5	4	6
− 3	7	3

_____ tickets

Spiral Review

Rewrite the subtraction. Find the difference.

5 $91 - 76 = \blacksquare$

6 $83 - 25 = \blacksquare$

LESSON 17.3
**More Practice/
Homework**

ONLINE
Video Tutorials and
Interactive Examples

Subtract Three-Digit Numbers

1 (MP) **Use Structure** Miguel scores
732 points on a video game.
Max scores 573 points. How
many more points does Miguel
score than Max? Solve. Show
your work.

Hundreds	Tens	Ones
	☐	
☐	☐	☐
7	3	2
− 5	7	3

Miguel scores _____ more points.

---

2 **Math on the Spot** Alex wrote this problem.
What are the missing digits?

Hundreds	Tens	Ones
7	13	
☐	☐	7
− 1	5	☐
6	8	1

Test Prep

3 Subtract. Fill in the bubble next to the correct answer.

○ 599

○ 601

○ 699

Hundreds	Tens	Ones
⬚	⬚	⬚
9	5	8
− 3	5	9

---

4 Mrs. Yo has 364 leaves. She uses 178 of the leaves in an art project. How many leaves does she have left?

Hundreds	Tens	Ones
⬚	⬚	⬚
3	6	4
− 1	7	8

_____ leaves

Spiral Review

Find the sum.

5

Hundreds	Tens	Ones
⬚	⬚	
4	9	8
+ 3	6	7

6

Hundreds	Tens	Ones
⬚	⬚	
3	5	8
+ 4	7	4

Represent Regrouping with Zeros

ⓂⓅ Attend to Precision Find the difference.
Show your work with a visual model.

ONLINE
Video Tutorials and
Interactive Examples

1 On Saturday, 700 people watched a race.
On Sunday, 562 people watched a race.
How many more people watched the
race on Saturday than on Sunday?

Hundreds	Tens	Ones
	☐	
☐	☐	☐
7	0	0
− 5	6	2

_____ more people

2 Mr. Finley's class uses 760 beans for art projects. Mrs. Huang's
class uses 589 beans. How many more beans does Mr. Finley's
class use than Mrs. Huang's class?

```
  7 | 6 | 0
− 5 | 8 | 9
```

_____ more beans

Subtract.

3
```
  4 | 0 | 0
− 1 | 2 | 0
```

4
```
  5 | 0 | 5
− 3 | 6 | 6
```

Test Prep

5 Eli read for 530 minutes this month. This is 145 more minutes than he read last month. How many minutes did Eli read last month?

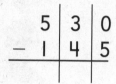

$$\begin{array}{c|c|c} 5 & 3 & 0 \\ \hline - 1 & 4 & 5 \\ \hline \end{array}$$

_____ minutes

---

6 Karima has 600 sheets of paper. She has 437 sheets of red paper. The other sheets of paper are blue. How many sheets of paper are blue?

$$\begin{array}{c|c|c} 6 & 0 & 0 \\ \hline - 4 & 3 & 7 \\ \hline \end{array}$$

_____ sheets of paper

Spiral Review

7 Kelly puts 3 strawberries, 5 blueberries, and 4 raspberries in her yogurt. How many berries does she use? Write an addition fact to show the problem. Circle two addends to add first. Write the sum. Solve.

_____ + _____ + _____ = _____

_____ berries

LESSON 17.5
**More Practice/
Homework**

ONLINE
Video Tutorials and
Interactive Examples

Regrouping with Zeros

Solve.

1 (MP) **Use Structure** There are 600 books and magazines in a library. There are 459 books. How many magazines are in the library?

```
  6 | 0 | 0
- 4 | 5 | 9
```

_____ magazines

2 (MP) **Reason** There are 440 paper clips in a box. There are 219 small paper clips. The rest of the paper clips are large. How many paper clips are large?

```
  4 | 4 | 0
- 2 | 1 | 9
```

_____ paper clips are large.

3 **Math on the Spot** Miguel has 125 more baseball cards than Chad. Miguel has 405 baseball cards. How many baseball cards does Chad have?

```
  4 | 0 | 5
- 1 | 2 | 5
```

_____ baseball cards

Subtract.

4
```
  6 | 0 | 6
- 2 | 9 | 9
```

5
```
  9 | 0 | 0
- 4 | 0 | 4
```

Test Prep

6 There are 700 rocks and shells. There are 438 rocks. How many shells are there? Fill in the bubble next to the correct answer.

○ 262

○ 272

○ 362

7 Samantha uses 770 beads on a project. Jack uses 568 beads. How many more beads does Samantha use than Jack?

```
  7 | 7 | 0
- 5 | 6 | 8
```

_____ more beads

Spiral Review

8 Mr. Mattel collects 340 shells. Show this number with a quick picture. Then write the number name.

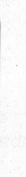

LESSON 17.6
**More Practice/
Homework**

ONLINE
Video Tutorials and
Interactive Examples

Add and Subtract Three-Digit Numbers

(MP) **Use Structure** Solve.

1 There are 800 napkins in a package. Students at
Falcon Elementary used 267 napkins during lunch.
How many napkins are left in the package?

```
    8  0  0
 -  2  6  7
```

There are _____ napkins left in the package.

2 On a bird watch, Mrs. Jacobs sees 258 birds.
Mrs. Martin sees 169 birds. How many birds
do they see altogether?

```
    2  5  8
 +  1  6  9
```

They see _____ birds altogether.

Solve. Remember to record any regrouping.

3
```
    3  9  8
 +  1  7  6
```

4
```
    7  0  7
 -  3  5  8
```

5
```
    8  0  0
 -  3  0  5
```

6
```
    4  2  0
 +  2  8  9
```

Test Prep

7 Mr. Zee has 259 tickets. He buys 179 more tickets. How many tickets does he have in all?

$$\begin{array}{r} 2\ 5\ 9 \\ +\ 1\ 7\ 9 \\ \hline \end{array}$$

He has ＿＿＿＿＿ tickets in all.

Fill in the bubble next to the correct answer.

8 On Saturday, 403 people go to a movie. On Sunday, 257 people go to a movie. How many more people go to a movie on Saturday than on Sunday?

$$\begin{array}{r} 4\ 0\ 3 \\ -\ 2\ 5\ 7 \\ \hline \end{array}$$

○ 154   ○ 660   ○ 146

9 Mrs. Thomas has 289 beads. She buys a box of 525 beads. How many beads does she have now?

$$\begin{array}{r} 2\ 8\ 9 \\ +\ 5\ 2\ 5 \\ \hline \end{array}$$

○ 236   ○ 814   ○ 704

Spiral Review

Write >, <, or = to compare the numbers.

10 560 ◯ 506

11 494 ◯ 449

12 700 ◯ 770

13 606 ◯ 665

Name _____

LESSON 18.1
**More Practice/
Homework**

ONLINE
Video Tutorials and
Interactive Examples

Estimate Lengths Using Inches

1 (MP) **Use Tools** Hans uses a tile that is 1 inch long to estimate length. Draw more tiles of the same size. What is the best estimate for the length of the paint set?

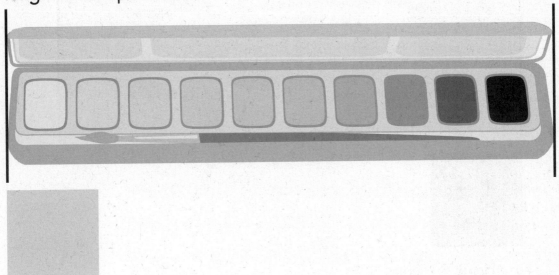

about _____ inches

---

2 **Math on the Spot** Use the tile. Estimate the length of each ribbon.

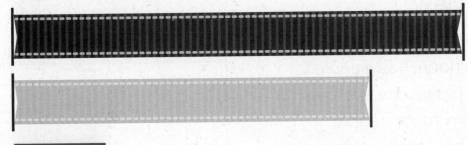

black ribbon: about _____ tiles long

gray ribbon: about _____ tiles long

Test Prep

3 The tile is 1 inch long. Which is the best estimate of the length of the tube of paint? Fill in the bubble next to the correct answer.

○ about 5 inches

○ about 7 inches

○ about 8 inches

Spiral Review

4 295 people saw a play in the afternoon. 432 people saw the play in the evening. How many more people saw the play in the evening than in the afternoon? Solve.

Hundreds	Tens	Ones
	☐	
☐	☐	☐
4	3	2
− 2	9	5

_____ more people

Name _____

LESSON 18.2
**More Practice/
Homework**

ONLINE
Video Tutorials and
Interactive Examples

Make and Use a Ruler

1 About how many inches long is the marker?

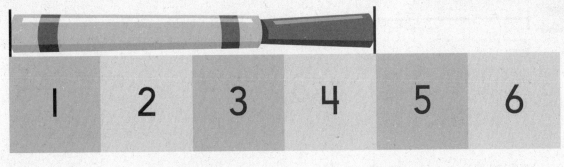

about _____ inches long

2 Explain how you can measure the ribbon using the paper ruler below.

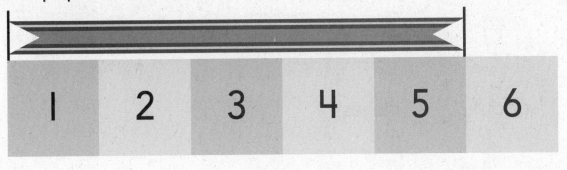

_____

_____

_____

3 Use one of your paper rulers. Draw a pencil that is 3 inches long.

Test Prep

Measure to the nearest inch.

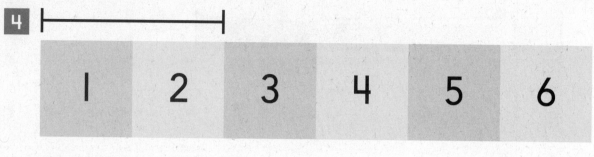

4

about _____ inches

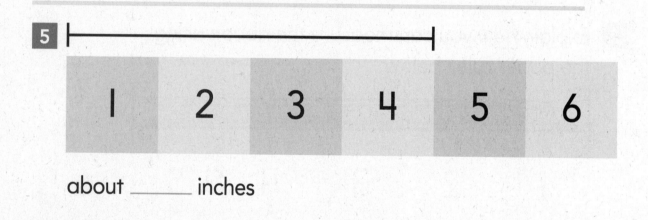

5

about _____ inches

Spiral Review

6 In an art store, there are 70 boxes of markers. There are 10 markers in each box. How many markers are in the art store?

_____ markers

7 Write <, >, or = to compare.

202 ◯ 212

Measure to the Nearest Inch

1 (MP) **Use Tools** Use a square tile and an inch ruler. Measure the length to the nearest inch.

_____ inches

2 (MP) **Use Tools** Lewis sees a worm on the ground. Measure the worm to the nearest inch with an inch ruler.

_____ inches

(MP) **Attend to Precision** Use an inch ruler to measure to the nearest inch.

3

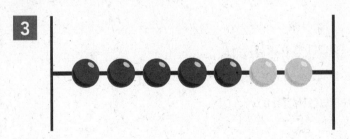

_____ inches

4

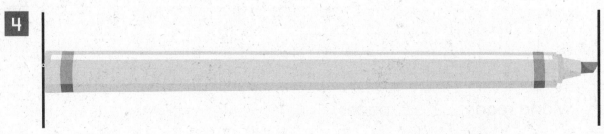

_____ inches

Test Prep

5 DeShawn finds a pinecone. Measure the pinecone to the nearest inch. Fill in the bubble next to the correct answer.

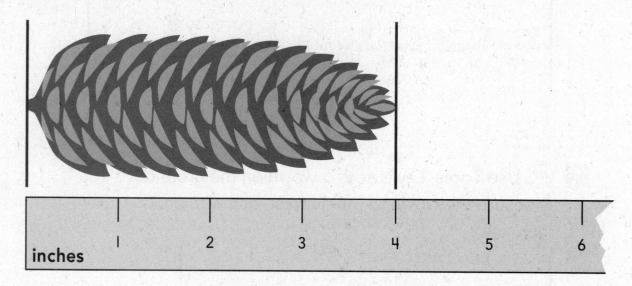

○ 3 inches

○ 4 inches

○ 5 inches

Spiral Review

6 Trevor reads 6 fewer pages than Malia. Trevor reads 15 pages. How many pages does Malia read? Write an equation to show the problem. Solve.

_____

_____

Maria reads _____ pages.

Make Line Plots to Show Measurement Data

1 **Math on the Spot** Use the data in the list to make a line plot.

Lengths of Ribbons
6 inches
5 inches
7 inches
6 inches

2 (MP) **Attend to Precision** Measure 3 pencils with an inch ruler. Record the lengths in inches.

Lengths of Pencils
_____ inches
_____ inches
_____ inches

3 Use the data from Problem 2 to make a line plot. Write a title. Label the line plot with numbers for the lengths. Draw an **X** on the line plot for each length.

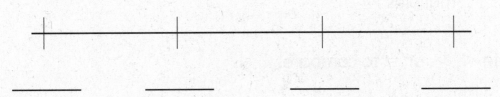

Test Prep

4 Omari made a line plot to show the lengths of some crayons. How many crayons are 4 inches long? Fill in the bubble next to the correct answer.

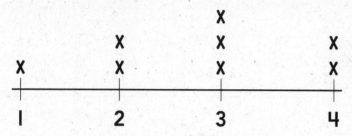

Lengths of Crayons in Inches

    ○ 1   ○ 2   ○ 3

---

5 Sasha measured the lengths of different books. She recorded the lengths. She will make a line plot to show the lengths. How many **X**s should Sasha draw above 8 on the line plot?

_____ **X**s

Lengths of Books
8 inches
5 inches
8 inches
9 inches
6 inches

Spiral Review

6 Stanley has 23 red marbles, 31 blue marbles, and 37 green marbles. How many marbles does he have in all?

_____ marbles

$$\begin{array}{r} 2\,|\,3 \\ 3\,|\,1 \\ +\ 3\,|\,7 \\ \hline \end{array}$$

7 Write <, >, or = to compare.

943 ◯ 493

Name _____

Estimate Lengths Using Feet

1 (MP) **Reason** Find a window. About how many feet long is the window?

Estimate: _____ feet

2 (MP) **Use Tools** Find a sign or poster. About how many feet long is the sign?

Estimate: _____ feet

3 (MP) **Reason** A bulletin board is about as long as 3 rulers. About how many feet long is the bulletin board?

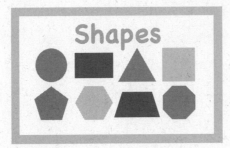

Estimate: _____ feet

4 Choose a large object in your home or classroom. Draw and label the object. Estimate its length in feet.

_____ feet

Test Prep

Fill in the bubble next to the correct answer.

5 Which is the best estimate for the length of a computer screen?

○ 1 foot   ○ 2 feet   ○ 6 feet

---

6 Which is the best estimate for the length of a couch?

○ 1 foot   ○ 3 feet   ○ 10 feet

Spiral Review

7 Use a hundred chart or a number line to solve.

$54 + 39 =$ _____

---

8 Andre has these coins. What is the total value of the coins?

_____

Name _____

LESSON 18.6
**More Practice/
Homework**

ONLINE
Video Tutorials and
Interactive Examples

Measure in Inches and Feet

1 **Use Tools** Use an inch ruler to measure the length of a banner or another large item to the nearest inch. Then measure its length to the nearest foot.

WELCOME TO 2ND GRADE!

_____ inches

_____ feet

---

2 Use an inch ruler to measure the length of a counter to the nearest inch. Then measure its length to the nearest foot.

_____ inches

_____ feet

---

3 Madison has a ribbon that is 6 feet long. Jason has a ribbon that is 6 inches long. Who has the shorter piece of ribbon? How do you know?

_____

_____

Test Prep

4 Write Inches or Feet to make the sentence true.

A jump rope is 6 _____ long.

A toy train is 10 _____ long.

A countertop is 60 _____ long.

5 Abby's string is 5 inches long. Isaiah's string is 5 feet long. Who has the longer string? Circle the correct answer.

Abby   Isaiah

Spiral Review

6 Harrison and Katie have 20 markers in all. They each have the same number of markers. How many markers do Harrison and Katie each have? Write an addition equation to show the equal groups. Solve.

_____ = _____ + _____   _____ markers

Write an addition equation to show the number as the sum of two equal addends.

7 12

_____ = _____ + _____

8 8

_____ = _____ + _____

© Houghton Mifflin Harcourt Publishing Company

LESSON 18.7
**More Practice/
Homework**

Ed **ONLINE**
Video Tutorials and
Interactive Examples

Measure to the Nearest Yard

1 (MP) **Reason** About how many yards long is a teacher's desk?

Estimate: _____ yards

2 Choose a large item. Estimate the length in yards.
Then measure the length in yards. Draw and label it.

Estimate: _____ yards

Measure: _____ yards

(MP) **Use Tools** Find each object. Use a yardstick to measure to the nearest yard. Write the length to the nearest yard.

3 mat

_____ yards

4 countertop

_____ yards

Test Prep

5 About how many yards long is a school bus? Fill in the bubble next to the correct answer.

○ 2 yards

○ 4 yards

○ 15 yards

6 How many 12-inch rulers are needed to match the length of 1 yardstick?

0 1 2 3 4 5 6 7 8 9 10 11 12 13 14 15 16 17 18 19 20 21 22 23 24 25 26 27 28 29 30 31 32 33 34 35 36
inches

_____ 12-inch rulers

7 Devin meaures a bike with a yardstick. About how many yards long is Devin's bike? Fill in the bubble next to the correct answer.

○ 1 yard   ○ 2 yards   ○ 5 yards

Spiral Review

8 Emma has 34 crayons. Tabitha has 28 crayons. How many crayons do they still need if they want a total of 70 crayons? Write two equations. Solve.

_____

_____

Emma and Tabitha still need _____ crayons.

Name _____

Choose Appropriate Tools

(MP) **Reason** Choose a tool and measure the object.

1 the length of a jump rope

Tool: _____

Length: _____

2 the distance around a basket

Tool: _____

Length: _____

3 Choose the best tool to measure the length of a stapler. Explain why you chose that tool.

_____

_____

_____

Test Prep

Fill in the bubble next to the correct answer.

4 Which is the best tool to measure the distance around a basketball?

○ inch ruler

○ yardstick

○ measuring tape

5 Jack needs to find the length of a snail for a science project. Which is the best tool to measure the length of a snail?

○ inch ruler

○ yardstick

○ measuring tape

Spiral Review

6 Stacy stacks 9 books. Then Stacy adds 8 more books to the stack. How many books are in the stack now? Make a ten to solve. Write the sum.

$9 + 8 =$ _____

$10 +$ _____ $=$ _____   _____ books

7 George catches 4 fish in the morning and 5 fish in the afternoon. How many fish does George catch? Write a doubles fact that can help you solve the problem. Solve.

_____ $+$ _____ $=$ _____   _____ fish

Estimate Lengths Using Centimeters

1 (MP) **Reason** The yarn is as long as 8 unit cubes. Which is the best estimate for the length of the paint set?

8 centimeters

10 centimeters

18 centimeters

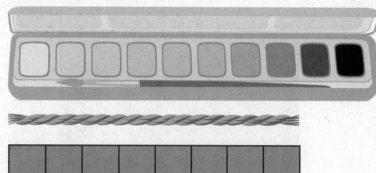

Math on the Spot The paper strip is 5 centimeters long. For each question, circle the best estimate.

2 About how long is the crayon?

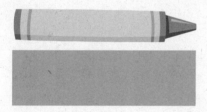

5 centimeters   10 centimeters   20 centimeters

3 About how long is the pencil?

10 centimeters

20 centimeters

40 centimeters

Test Prep

4 Percy knows the crayon is 5 centimeters long. Which is the best estimate for the length of the notebook using Percy's crayon?

○ about 5 centimeters

○ about 10 centimeters

○ about 15 centimeters

Spiral Review

5 Find the sum.

Hundreds	Tens	Ones
☐		
5	3	6
+ 3	8	2

6 Which unit is shorter, one inch or one foot?

LESSON 19.2
**More Practice/
Homework**

ONLINE
Video Tutorials and
Interactive Examples

Measure to the Nearest Centimeter

(MP) **Use Tools Measure the length to the nearest centimeter.**

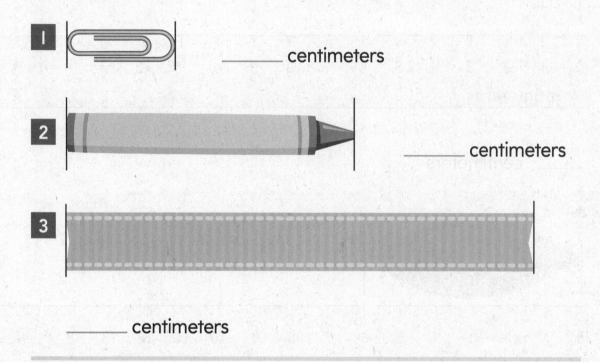

1. _____ centimeters

2. _____ centimeters

3. _____ centimeters

---

4. **Open Ended** Hannah says the crayon is 12 centimeters long. Is she correct? Explain.

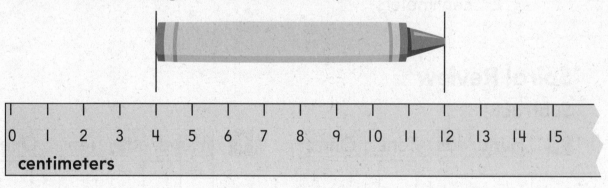

_____

_____

Test Prep

Measure each object to the nearest centimeter.

5

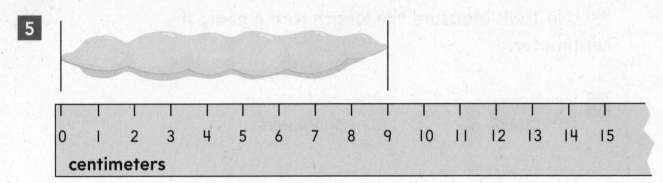

_____ centimeters

6

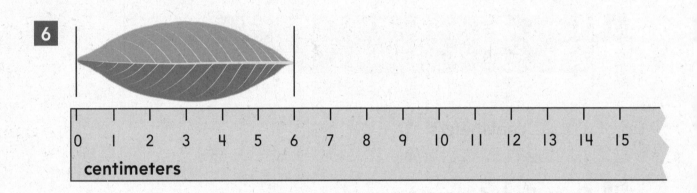

_____ centimeters

Spiral Review

Subtract.

7

Hundreds	Tens	Ones
	☐	☐
5	3	4
− 2	2	8

8

Hundreds	Tens	Ones
	☐	☐
4	5	1
− 3	6	8

LESSON 19.3
**More Practice/
Homework**

ONLINE
Video Tutorials and
Interactive Examples

Estimate Lengths Using Meters

(MP) **Use Structure Find the real object.
Estimate its length in meters.**

1 a bookcase

about _____ meter

2 a rug

about _____ meters

3 Find an object that you would estimate has a length
of about 3 meters. Draw and label the object.

Test Prep

Fill in the bubble next to the correct answer.

4 Which is the best estimate for the length of a classroom board?

- ○ 2 meters
- ○ 4 meters
- ○ 6 meters

5 Which is the best estimate for the length of a bicycle?

- ○ 2 meters
- ○ 7 meters
- ○ 15 meters

Spiral Review

6 Use an inch ruler to measure the length of the pencil.

_____ inches

7 Which measurement of a table is greater, the number of feet or the number of inches?

_____

LESSON 19.4
**More Practice/
Homework**

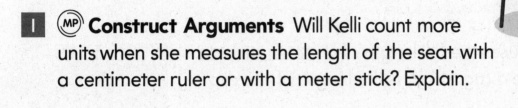 **ONLINE**
Video Tutorials and
Interactive Examples

Measure in Centimeters and Meters

Kelli measures the chair seat with a centimeter ruler and with a meter stick. How are the units different in the two measurements?

1 (MP) **Construct Arguments** Will Kelli count more units when she measures the length of the seat with a centimeter ruler or with a meter stick? Explain.

_____

_____

_____

_____

Choose the best tool to use. Then measure the length of the real object.

2

Windows

centimeter ruler

meter stick

_____ centimeters

_____ meters

3

Frame

centimeter ruler

meter stick

_____ centimeters

_____ meters

Test Prep

4 Which is the best tool to use to measure the length of a glove?

centimeter ruler   meter stick

5 Sandra uses the full length of 2 meter sticks to measure a rug. What is the length of the rug?

_____ meters

Spiral Review

6 Use the data in the list to label the line plot with a title and numbers for the lengths. Draw an **X** on the line plot for each length.

Lengths of Leaves
3 inches
5 inches
4 inches
6 inches
5 inches

| | | | |

_____   _____   _____   _____

_____

LESSON 20.1
**More Practice/
Homework**

ONLINE
Video Tutorials and
Interactive Examples

Relate Inches to a Number Line

1 (MP) **Reason** Brody has 24 leaves. The wind
blows away 14 leaves. How many leaves does
Brody have now?

Show your work on the yardstick and complete
the equation.

_____ − _____ = _____

Brody has _____ leaves now.

2 (MP) **Reason** Explain how you used the yardstick to
solve Problem 1.

_____

_____

_____

Use the yardstick to solve.

3 36 − 14 = _____

4 _____ = 33 − 12

5 23 + 13 = _____

6 11 + 22 = _____

Test Prep

Solve.

7 Mark has 16 sports cards. His father gives him 13 more sports cards. How many sports cards does Mark have now?

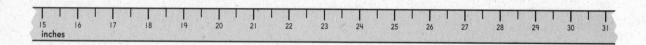

_____ sports cards

---

8 14 + 14 = _____

Spiral Review

9 Show the number 862 in three ways.

_____ hundreds _____ tens _____ ones

Expanded form: _____

Write the number name.

_____

LESSON 20.2
**More Practice/
Homework**

ONLINE
Video Tutorials and
Interactive Examples

Add and Subtract Lengths
in Inches

**Write an equation using ▨ for the unknown
number. Use the number line to solve.**

1 (MP) **Use Structure** Cristina has a toy boat that
is 13 inches long. Manny has a toy boat that is
15 inches long. How long are both boats together?

_____

Both boats together are _____ inches long.

---

2 **Math on the Spot** Sue has 2 ribbons that have
the same length. She has 18 inches of ribbon in all.
How long is each ribbon?

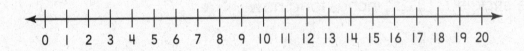

_____

Each ribbon is _____ inches long.

Test Prep

Write an equation using ■ for the unknown number. Solve.

3 Polly makes a paper clip chain that is 8 inches long. She wants it to be 24 inches long. How many more inches does Polly need to add to the paper clip chain?

0 1 2 3 4 5 6 7 8 9 10 11 12 13 14 15 16 17 18 19 20 21 22 23 24 25

_____

Polly needs to add _____ more inches.

4 Valeri finds a stick that is 18 inches long. Then 5 inches break off of the stick. How long is the stick now?

0 1 2 3 4 5 6 7 8 9 10 11 12 13 14 15 16 17 18 19 20 21 22 23 24 25

_____

The stick is _____ inches long now.

Spiral Review

Solve.

5 Annie has these coins. What is the total value of her coins?

_____

© Houghton Mifflin Harcourt Publishing Company

Name _____

LESSON 20.3
**More Practice/
Homework**

ONLINE
Video Tutorials and
Interactive Examples

Relate Centimeters to a Number Line

1 (MP) **Construct Arguments** Liam is making a number line. Show Liam how to fix his mistakes. Write the correct numbers above the number line.

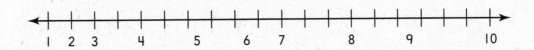

Explain how you know your work is correct.

_____

_____

_____

(MP) **Use Structure** Use a centimeter ruler or a meter stick to solve.

2 A duck walks 27 centimeters. Another duck walks 15 centimeters. How many centimeters do the ducks walk in all?

_____ centimeters

3 Mrs. Hunt has a wire 47 centimeters long. She cuts some of the wire to use. The wire is now 19 centimeters long. How many centimeters of wire did Mrs. Hunt cut?

_____ centimeters

Test Prep

4 Sara is making a chain of paper rings. Her chain is 7 centimeters long. She wants it to be 15 centimeters long. How many centimeters does Sara need to add to her chain?

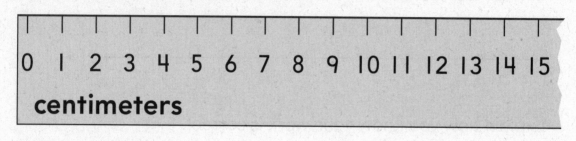

_____ centimeters

Spiral Review

Use the picture graph to solve the problems.

Toys in a Toy Box					
puzzles	☺	☺	☺		
trains	☺	☺	☺	☺	
animals	☺	☺	☺	☺	☺
dolls	☺	☺	☺	☺	

Key: Each ☺ stands for 1 toy.

5 How many toys are in the toy box?   _____ toys

6 How many more animals than puzzles are in the toy box?   _____ more animals

LESSON 20.4
**More Practice/
Homework**

Ed **ONLINE**
Video Tutorials and
Interactive Examples

Add and Subtract Lengths
in Centimeters

1 **(MP) Reason** A stick is 24 centimeters long.
Haji breaks it into two pieces. One piece is
15 centimeters long. How long is the other piece?
Write an equation using ▆ for the unknown
number. Use the number line to solve.

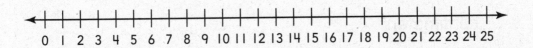

_____

_____ centimeters

---

2 **Math on the Spot** A chalk line was 23 centimeters long.
Then Greg erased part of the line. Now the chalk line
is 6 centimeters long. How many centimeters of the
line did Greg erase?

Greg erased _____ centimeters of the chalk line.

Test Prep

Write an equation using ■ for the unknown number. Solve.

3 A carrot is 12 centimeters long. It grows 12 more centimeters. How long is the carrot now?

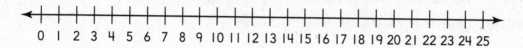

_____

_____ centimeters

4 Ronan has a ribbon that is 22 centimeters long. He cuts part of the ribbon. Now it is 14 centimeters long. How many centimeters does he cut?

_____

_____ centimeters

Spiral Review

Write the time in different ways.

5

_____ : _____

_____ minutes after _____

Name _____

LESSON 20.5
**More Practice/
Homework**

ONLINE
Video Tutorials and
Interactive Examples

Measure and Compare Lengths in Centimeters

1 (MP) **Use Tools** Measure the length of each object.
Write an equation to find the difference. Compare
the lengths.

_____ centimeters

_____ centimeters

_____

The black ribbon is _____ centimeters _____
than the gray ribbon.

---

2 **Math on the Spot** Use a centimeter ruler.
Measure the length of a desk and the length of
a book.

desk: _____ centimeters

book: _____ centimeters

Which is shorter? _____

How much shorter is it? _____ centimeters

Test Prep

3 Which describes the lengths of the paper clip and the yarn? Fill in the bubble next to the correct answer.

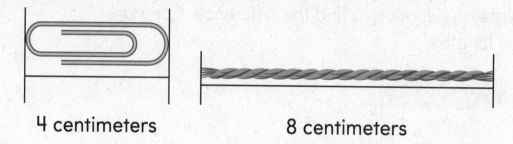

4 centimeters   8 centimeters

○ The paper clip is 8 centimeters longer than the yarn.

○ The paper clip is 4 centimeters shorter than the yarn.

○ The yarn is 8 centimeters longer than the paper clip.

Spiral Review

4 Paul has 12 yellow flowers and 15 red flowers. He gives 6 flowers to Laura. How many flowers does he have left? Write two equations. Solve.

_____

_____

Paul has _____ flowers left.

Add or subtract.

5

Hundreds	Tens	Ones
☐	☐	
3	4	7
+ 2	1	5

6

Hundreds	Tens	Ones
☐	☐	
6	3	8
− 1	8	4

Name _____

LESSON 21.1
More Practice/ Homework

ONLINE
Video Tutorials and
Interactive Examples

Identify and Draw Three-Dimensional Shapes

1 (MP) **Construct Arguments** What is the name of this shape? How do you know?

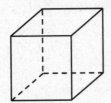

_____

_____

2 **Math on the Spot** These are all the faces of a rectangular prism. Write to tell about the shapes.

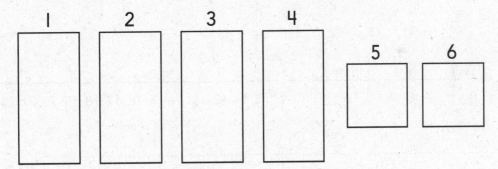

_____

_____

3 (MP) **Use Repeated Reasoning** How many faces, edges, and vertices does a cube have?

_____ faces

_____ edges

_____ vertices

Test Prep

4 Which names the number of edges of a rectangular prism? Fill in the bubble next to the correct answer.

○ 4

○ 8

○ 12

Spiral Review

Use a number line to draw a visual model.
Write an equation to represent and solve the problem.

5 Ray has 21 centimeters of string. He gives 8 centimeters of string to Kevin. How many centimeters of string does Ray have now?

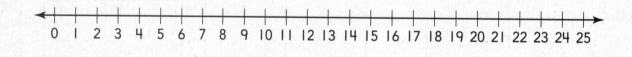

_____ centimeters

6 Matt has 6 inches of yarn. His mother gives him 14 more inches of yarn. How many inches of yarn does Matt have now?

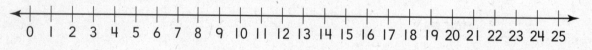

_____ inches

LESSON 21.2
**More Practice/
Homework**

ONLINE
Video Tutorials and
Interactive Examples

Identify and Draw
Two-Dimensional Shapes

Solve.

1 **Math on the Spot** Alex draws a quadrilateral
and two pentagons. How many sides does Alex
draw altogether?

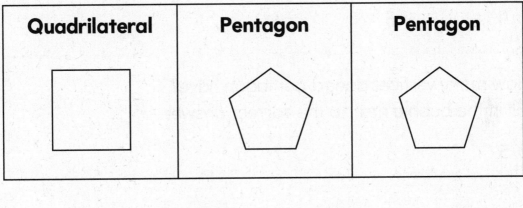

| Quadrilateral | Pentagon | Pentagon |

_____ sides + _____ sides + _____ sides = _____ sides

Alex draws _____ sides altogether.

---

2 **(MP)** **Reason** Sasha draws a picture of a hexagon. Zeke
draws a picture of a triangle. How many more vertices
does Sasha's shape have than Zeke's shape?

_____ more vertices

3 **(MP)** **Use Structure** Carla has a pentagon and a
hexagon. Which shape has more vertices?

| hexagon | pentagon | quadrilateral | triangle |

_____

Test Prep

4 How many vertices does a quadrilateral have?
Fill in the bubble next to the correct answer.

○ 3   ○ 4   ○ 5

5 How many sides does a hexagon have? Fill in the
bubble next to the correct answer.

○ 4   ○ 5   ○ 6

6 How many vertices does a pentagon have?
Fill in the bubble next to the correct answer.

○ 5   ○ 6   ○ 7

Spiral Review

7 Measure each object and write an equation to find
the difference. Compare the lengths.

The pencil is _____ centimeters long.

The pen is _____ centimeters long.

_____

Which object is longer? _____

Find and Count Angles in Two-Dimensional Shapes

1 **Math on the Spot** Draw more sides to make the shape. Write how many angles.

pentagon

quadrilateral

_____ angles

_____ angles

---

2 **(MP) Use Structure** Write the number of angles in each shape.

triangle: _____ angles

hexagon: _____ angles

pentagon: _____ angles

quadrilateral: _____ angles

---

3 **(MP) Reason** Bryson draws 2 two-dimensional shapes that have 7 angles in all. Draw 2 shapes Bryson could have drawn.

Test Prep

4 How many angles are in the shape?
Fill in the bubble next to the correct answer.

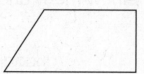

○ 3

○ 4

○ 5

---

5 How many angles does a pentagon have?
Fill in the bubble next to the correct answer.

○ 4

○ 5

○ 6

---

6 Melanie draws a shape with 5 sides and 5 angles.
What shape does she draw? Fill in the bubble
next to the correct answer.

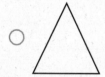 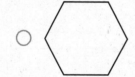 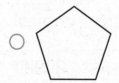

Spiral Review

7 How many vertices does a rectangular prism have?

_____ vertices

---

8 How many more sides does a hexagon have than
a quadrilateral?

_____ more sides

LESSON 21.4
**More Practice/
Homework**

ONLINE
Video Tutorials and
Interactive Examples

Sort Two-Dimensional Shapes by Sides and Angles

1 **Math on the Spot** Draw three shapes with fewer than 5 angles. Circle the angles. Then draw two shapes with 5 or more angles. Circle the angles.

Shapes with fewer than 5 angles	Shapes with 5 or more angles

2 **Open Ended** Isabella drew a shape with more than 3 angles. It is not a hexagon. Draw and name the shape Isabella may have drawn. Then write the number of angles and sides in the shape.

shape: _____   _____ angles   _____ sides

�circledMP **Attend to Precision** Draw two shapes that match the rule.

3 Shapes with more than 4 angles

4 Shapes with fewer than 5 sides

Test Prep

Choose the two correct answers.

5 Which shapes have fewer than 5 angles?

- ○ quadrilateral
- ○ triangle
- ○ hexagon
- ○ pentagon

6 Which shapes have more than 4 sides?

- ○ rectangle
- ○ triangle
- ○ hexagon
- ○ pentagon

Spiral Review

7 Which three-dimensional shape has only square faces?

cube	rectangular prism

_____

8 Which two-dimensional shape has 6 vertices?

hexagon	pentagon	quadrilateral	triangle

_____

LESSON 22.1
**More Practice/
Homework**

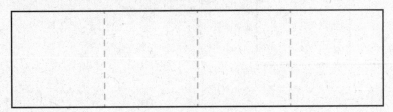

ONLINE
Video Tutorials and
Interactive Examples

Partition Rectangles

1 (MP) **Use Tools** Use color tiles to
cover this rectangle. Write how many.

How many rows? _____

How many columns? _____

How many square tiles? _____

---

2 (MP) **Reason** Jake wants to cover this rectangle
with color tiles. There are 4 rows and
3 columns. How many square tiles are there?

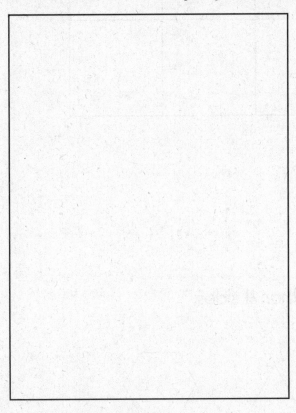

_____ square tiles

Test Prep

3 Look at the rectangle. Write how many.

How many rows? _____

How many columns? _____

How many square tiles? _____

---

4 How many rows and columns are there in the rectangle?
Fill in the bubble next to the correct answer.

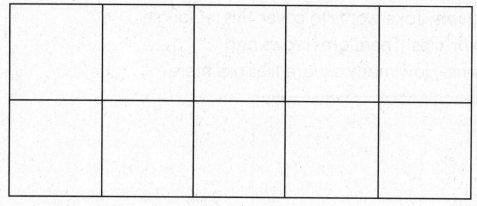

○ 2 rows and 5 columns

○ 5 rows and 3 columns

○ 2 rows and 4 columns

Spiral Review

5 Circle the shapes with more than 4 sides.

© Houghton Mifflin Harcourt Publishing Company

Name _____

LESSON 22.2
**More Practice/
Homework**

Ed **ONLINE**
Video Tutorials and
Interactive Examples

Identify and Describe
Equal Shares

(MP) **Use Structure** Write *halves*, *thirds*, or
fourths to name the equal shares.

1

_____

2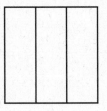

_____

3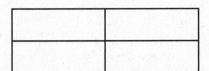

_____

(MP) **Reason** Write the number of equal shares. Then
write *halves*, *thirds*, or *fourths* to name the shares.

4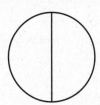

_____ equal shares

_____

5

_____ equal shares

_____

Test Prep

Fill in the bubble next to the correct answer.

6 Which has 4 equal shares?

○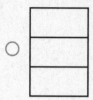

○

○

---

7 Which names the equal shares?

○ halves   ○ thirds   ○ fourths

Spiral Review

8 Write how many.

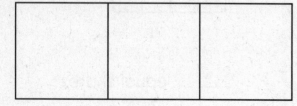

How many rows? _____

How many columns? _____

How many square tiles? _____

LESSON 22.3
**More Practice/
Homework**

 **ONLINE**
Video Tutorials and
Interactive Examples

Draw Equal Shares

1 Luis wants to cut a pizza into equal shares.
Draw to show how he could cut the pizza.

halves	thirds	fourths
◯	◯	◯

2 (MP) **Reason** Bella says this square shows halves.
Is she correct? Explain.

_____

_____

(MP) **Attend to Precision** Draw to show equal shares.

3 halves   **4** thirds   **5** fourths

Test Prep

6 Which shapes show fourths?
Choose the two correct answers.

○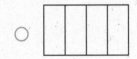

○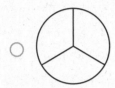

○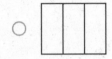

○

Spiral Review

Find the real object. Estimate its length in meters.

7 About how long is a table?

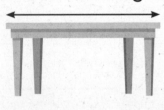

about _____ meters

8 About how long is a chair?

about _____ meter

Show and Describe an Equal Share

1 Draw to show thirds. Color a third of the shape.

(MP) **Reason** Color 1 equal share blue. Then write *half of*, *third of*, or *fourth of* to name the blue share.

2

A _____ the square is blue.

3

A _____ the circle is blue.

(MP) **Use Structure** Draw and color to show an equal share of the shape.

4 A quarter of the circle is red.

5 A half of the rectangle is red.

Test Prep

6 Which sentence names the shaded share of the circle?
Fill in the bubble next to the correct answer.

○ A half of the circle is shaded.

○ A third of the circle is shaded.

○ A fourth of the circle is shaded.

7 Which rectangle has a fourth shaded gray? Fill in the
bubble next to the correct answer.

○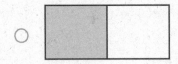

○

○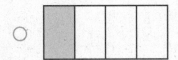

Spiral Review

8 Estimate the length of the window in yards.

about _____ yard

9 Write *halves*, *thirds*, or *fourths* to name
the equal shares.

_____

Name _____

LESSON 22.5
**More Practice/
Homework**

ONLINE
Video Tutorials and
Interactive Examples

Different Ways to Show Equal Shares

1 **Math on the Spot** Erin has two ribbons that are the same size. What are two different ways she can cut the ribbons into thirds?

2 Draw two different ways to show fourths.

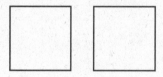

3 Draw two different ways you can fold a paper into halves.

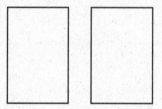

4 **(MP)** **Use Structure** Use your drawings to compare the halves in the two rectangles.

_____

_____

_____

Test Prep

5 Randy is sharing a cracker with his friend. Which crackers show halves? Choose the two correct answers.

○

○

○

○

Spiral Review

Subtract.

6
```
    7 0 3
  - 2 5 8
```

7
```
    4 2 0
  - 1 3 9
```

8
```
    6 0 0
  - 3 2 2
```

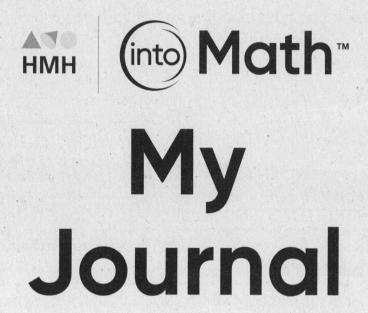

My Journal

My Progress on Mathematics Standards

The lessons in your *Into Math* book provide instruction for Mathematics Standards for Grade 2. You can use the following pages to reflect on your learning and record your progress through the standards.

As you learn new concepts, reflect on this learning. Consider inserting a check mark if you understand the concepts or inserting a question mark if you have questions or need help.

	Student Edition Lessons	My Progress
Domain OPERATIONS AND ALGEBRAIC THINKING		
Cluster 1: Represent and solve problems involving addition and subtraction.		
Use addition and subtraction within 100 to solve one- and two-step word problems involving situations of adding to, taking from, putting together, taking apart, and comparing, with unknowns in all positions, e.g., by using drawings and equations with a symbol for the unknown number to represent the problem.	14.1, 14.2, 14.3, 14.4, 15.1, 15.2, 15.3	
Cluster 2: Add and subtract within 20.		
Fluently add and subtract within 20 using mental strategies. By end of Grade 2, know from memory all sums of two one-digit numbers.	1.1, 1.2, 1.3, 1.4, 1.5, 1.6, 1.7	

	Student Edition Lessons	My Progress
Cluster 3: Work with equal groups of objects to gain foundations for multiplication.		
Determine whether a group of objects (up to 20) has an odd or even number of members, e.g., by pairing objects or counting them by 2s; write an equation to express an even number as a sum of two equal addends.	2.1, 2.2	
Use addition to find the total number of objects arranged in rectangular arrays with up to 5 rows and up to 5 columns; write an equation to express the total as a sum of equal addends.	2.3, 2.4, 2.5	
Domain NUMBER AND OPERATIONS IN BASE TEN		
Cluster 1: Understand place value.		
Understand that the three digits of a three-digit number represent amounts of hundreds, tens, and ones; e.g., 706 equals 7 hundreds, 0 tens, and 6 ones. Understand the following as special cases:	4.2, 4.3, 4.4, 4.5	
• 100 can be thought of as a bundle of ten tens — called a "hundred."	4.1	
• The numbers 100, 200, 300, 400, 500, 600, 700, 800, 900 refer to one, two, three, four, five, six, seven, eight, or nine hundreds (and 0 tens and 0 ones).	4.1	
Count within 1000; skip-count by 5s, 10s, and 100s.	6.1	

Interactive Standards

	Student Edition Lessons	My Progress
Read and write numbers to 1000 using base-ten numerals, number names, and expanded form.	4.4, 5.1, 5.2, 5.3, 5.4, 5.5	
Compare two three-digit numbers based on meanings of the hundreds, tens, and ones digits, using >, =, and < symbols to record the results of comparisons.	6.4, 6.5	
Cluster 2: Use place value understanding and properties of operations to add and subtract.		
Fluently add and subtract within 100 using strategies based on place value, properties of operations, and/or the relationship between addition and subtraction.	10.1, 10.2, 10.3, 11.1, 11.2, 11.3, 11.4, 11.5, 12.1, 12.2, 12.3, 12.4, 12.5, 12.6, 13.1, 13.2, 13.3, 13.4, 13.5	
Add up to four two-digit numbers using strategies based on place value and properties of operations.	13.3, 13.4, 13.5	

Interactive Standards

	Student Edition Lessons	My Progress
Add and subtract within 1000, using concrete models or drawings and strategies based on place value, properties of operations, and/or the relationship between addition and subtraction; relate the strategy to a written method. Understand that in adding or subtracting three-digit numbers, one adds or subtracts hundreds and hundreds, tens and tens, ones and ones; and sometimes it is necessary to compose or decompose tens or hundreds.	13.3, 13.4, 13.5, 16.1, 16.2, 16.3, 16.4, 17.1, 17.2, 17.3, 17.4, 17.5, 17.6	
Mentally add 10 or 100 to a given number 100–900, and mentally subtract 10 or 100 from a given number 100–900.	6.2, 6.3	
Explain why addition and subtraction strategies work, using place value and the properties of operations.	12.5, 12.6, 13.3, 13.4, 13.5, 17.3	
Domain MEASUREMENT AND DATA		
Cluster 1: Measure and estimate lengths in standard units.		
Measure the length of an object by selecting and using appropriate tools such as rulers, yardsticks, meter sticks, and measuring tapes.	18.2, 18.3, 18.7, 18.8, 19.2	
Measure the length of an object twice, using length units of different lengths for the two measurements; describe how the two measurements relate to the size of the unit chosen.	18.6, 19.4	

	Student Edition Lessons	My Progress
Estimate lengths using units of inches, feet, centimeters, and meters.	18.1, 18.5, 19.1, 19.3	
Measure to determine how much longer one object is than another, expressing the length difference in terms of a standard length unit.	20.5	
Cluster 2: Relate addition and subtraction to length.		
Use addition and subtraction within 100 to solve word problems involving lengths that are given in the same units, e.g., by using drawings (such as drawings of rulers) and equations with a symbol for the unknown number to represent the problem.	20.2, 20.4	
Represent whole numbers as lengths from 0 on a number line diagram with equally spaced points corresponding to the numbers 0, 1, 2, ..., and represent whole-number sums and differences within 100 on a number line diagram.	20.1, 20.2, 20.3, 20.4	
Cluster 3: Work with time and money.		
Tell and write time from analog and digital clocks to the nearest five minutes, using a.m. and p.m.	9.1, 9.2, 9.3, 9.4	
Solve word problems involving dollar bills, quarters, dimes, nickels, and pennies, using $ and ¢ symbols appropriately. Example: If you have 2 dimes and 3 pennies, how many cents do you have?	7.1, 7.2, 7.3, 7.4, 8.1, 8.2, 8.3	

	Student Edition Lessons	My Progress
Cluster 4: Represent and interpret data.		
Generate measurement data by measuring lengths of several objects to the nearest whole unit, or by making repeated measurements of the same object. Show the measurements by making a line plot, where the horizontal scale is marked off in whole-number units.	18.4	
Draw a picture graph and a bar graph (with single-unit scale) to represent a data set with up to four categories. Solve simple put-together, take-apart, and compare problems using information presented in a bar graph.	3.1, 3.2, 3.3, 3.4, 3.5	
Domain GEOMETRY		
Cluster 1: Reason with shapes and their attributes.		
Recognize and draw shapes having specified attributes, such as a given number of angles or a given number of equal faces. Identify triangles, quadrilaterals, pentagons, hexagons, and cubes.	21.1, 21.2, 21.3, 21.4	
Partition a rectangle into rows and columns of same-size squares and count to find the total number of them.	22.1	
Partition circles and rectangles into two, three, or four equal shares, describe the shares using the words *halves*, *thirds*, *half of*, *a third of*, etc., and describe the whole as two halves, three thirds, four fourths. Recognize that equal shares of identical wholes need not have the same shape.	22.2, 22.3, 22.4, 22.5	

My Learning Summary

As you learn about new concepts, complete a learning summary for each module. A learning summary can include drawings, examples, non-examples, and terminology. It's your learning summary, so show or include information that will help you.

At the end of each module, you will have a summary you can reference to review content for a module test and help you make connections with related math concepts.

My Learning Summary

My Learning Summary

My Learning Summary

My Learning Summary

My Learning Summary

My Learning Summary

My Learning Summary

My Learning Summary

My Learning Summary

My Learning Summary

My Learning Summary

My Learning Summary

My Learning Summary

My Learning Summary

My Learning Summary

My Learning Summary

My Learning Summary

My Learning Summary

My Learning Summary

My Learning Summary

My Learning Summary

My Learning Summary

As you learn about each new term, add notes, drawings, or sentences in the space next to the definition. Doing so will help you remember what each term means.

A

My Vocabulary Summary

addend
sumando

$$5 + 8 = 13$$

addends

addition equation
ecuación de suma

$$5 + 7 = 12$$
$$14 = 8 + 6$$

a.m.
a. m.

Times after midnight and before noon are written with **a.m.**

11:00 a.m. is in the morning.

angle
ángulo

angle

B

My Vocabulary Summary

bar graph
gráfica de barras

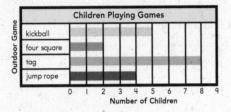

C

centimeter
centímetro

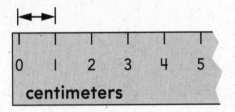

centimeter ruler
regla de centímetros

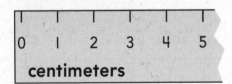

A **centimeter ruler** is a tool used to measure the length of an object in centimeter units.

My Vocabulary Summary

cent sign
signo de centavo

68¢

cent sign

compare
comparar

Use these symbols when you **compare**: >, <, =.

241 > 234

123 < 128

247 = 247

compare
comparar

Compare the lengths of the pencil and the crayon.

The pencil is longer than the crayon.

The crayon is shorter than the pencil.

Interactive Glossary

My Vocabulary Summary

data
datos

Data is another word for information.

decimal point
punto decimal

$1.00

↑

decimal point

difference
diferencia

9 − 2 = 7

↑

difference

dime
moneda de 10¢

A **dime** has a value of 10 cents.

My Vocabulary Summary

dollar
dólar

One **dollar** is worth 100 cents.

dollar sign
signo de dólar

$1.00

↑

dollar sign

doubles
dobles

2   +   2   =   4

E

My Vocabulary Summary

edge
arista

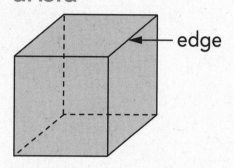

An **edge** is formed where two faces of a three-dimensional shape meet.

estimate
estimar

To **estimate** is to make a reasonable guess.

even
par

2, 4, 6, 8, 10, . . .

F

My Vocabulary Summary

face
cara

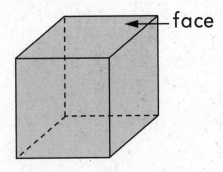
face

Each flat surface of this cube is a **face**.

foot
pie

1 **foot** is the same length as 12 inches.

fourth of
cuarto de

A **fourth of** the shape is shaded.

fourths
cuartos

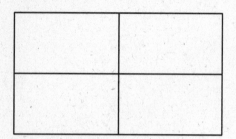

This shape has 4 equal parts.

These equal parts are called **fourths.**

G

greatest value
mayor valor

A coin with the **greatest value** is worth the largest amount.

| **H** | **My Vocabulary Summary** |

half of
mitad de

A **half of** the shape is shaded.

half past
y media

2:30

30 minutes after 2
half past 2

halves
mitades

This shape has 2 equal parts. These equal parts are called **halves**.

Interactive Glossary

My Vocabulary Summary

height
altura

Height is a length that is measured from top to bottom.

hexagon
hexágono

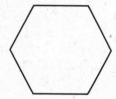

A two-dimensional shape with 6 sides is a **hexagon**.

hour
hora

There are 60 minutes in 1 **hour**.

hundred
centena

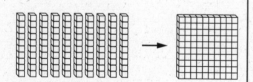

There are 10 tens in 1 **hundred**.

I

inch
pulgada

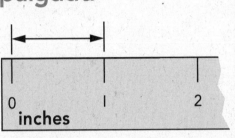

inch ruler
regla de pulgadas

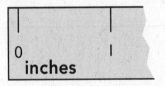

is equal to (=)
es igual a

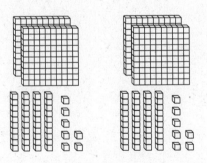

247 is equal to 247.
247 = 247

My Vocabulary Summary

is greater than (>)
es mayor que

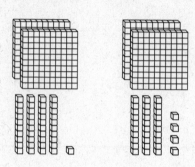

241 is greater than 234.

241 > 234

is less than (<)
es menor que

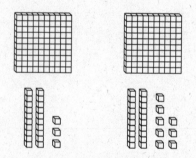

123 is less than 128.

123 < 128

K

key
clave

Number of Soccer Games							
March	⚽	⚽	⚽	⚽			
April	⚽	⚽	⚽				
May	⚽	⚽	⚽	⚽	⚽	⚽	
June	⚽	⚽	⚽	⚽	⚽	⚽	⚽

Key: Each ⚽ stands for 1 game.

The **key** tells how many each picture stands for.

L

least value
menor valor

A coin with the **least value** is worth the smallest amount.

line plot
diagrama de puntos

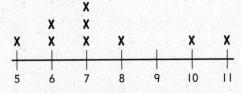

Lengths of Paintbrushes in Inches

A **line plot** shows data on a number line.

M

measure

medir

To **measure** length is to find how long an object is in units such as inches or centimeters.

measuring tape

cinta métrica

A **measuring tape** can bend to measure lengths that are not flat or straight.

meter

metro

1 **meter** is the same length as 100 centimeters.

meter stick

regla de un metro

A **meter stick** is a measurement tool with a length of 1 meter.

My Vocabulary Summary

midnight

medianoche

Midnight is 12:00 at night.

minute

minuto

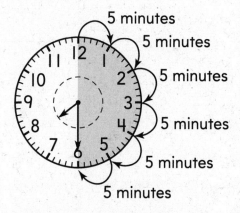

There are 30 **minutes** in a half hour.

N

nickel

moneda de 5¢

A **nickel** has a value of 5 cents.

Interactive Glossary

noon

mediodía

Noon is 12:00 in the daytime.

O

odd

impar

1, 3, 5, 7, 9, 11, . . .

odd numbers

operation

operación

Addition and subtraction are **operations**.

21 + 42 = 63

63 − 21 = 42

| P | My Vocabulary Summary |

pattern
patrón

45, 50, 55, 60, 65, 70, 75

A **pattern** is something that repeats in the same way.

penny
moneda de 1¢

A **penny** has a value of 1 cent.

pentagon
pentágono

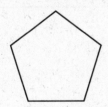

A two-dimensional shape with 5 sides is a **pentagon**.

My Vocabulary Summary

picture graph
pictografía

Number of Soccer Games							
March	⚽	⚽	⚽	⚽			
April	⚽	⚽	⚽				
May	⚽	⚽	⚽	⚽	⚽	⚽	
June	⚽	⚽	⚽	⚽	⚽	⚽	⚽

Key: Each ⚽ stands for 1 game.

p.m.
p. m.

Times after noon and before midnight are written with **p.m.**

11:00 p.m. is in the evening.

Q

quadrilateral
cuadrilátero

A two-dimensional shape with 4 sides is a **quadrilateral.**

My Vocabulary Summary

quarter
moneda de 25¢

A **quarter** has a value of 25 cents.

quarter of
un cuarto de

A **quarter of** this shape is shaded.

quarter past
y cuarto

15 minutes after 8
quarter past 8

Glossary

Interactive Glossary

R

regroup
reagrupar

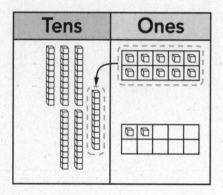

You can trade 10 ones for
1 ten to **regroup**.

related facts
operaciones relacionadas

$$7 + 5 = 12 \quad 5 + 7 = 12$$
$$12 - 5 = 7 \quad 12 - 7 = 5$$

ruler
regla

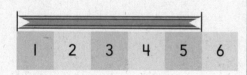

A **ruler** is a tool used to
measure length.

S

side
lado

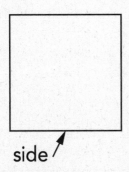

side

This shape has 4 **sides**.

sum
suma o total

$$9 + 6 = 15$$

sum

survey
encuesta

Favorite Lunch	
Lunch	Tally
pizza	IIII
sandwich	IIII I
salad	III
pasta	IIII

A **survey** is a collection of data from answers to a question.

T

third of
tercio de

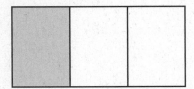

A **third of** the shape is shaded.

thirds
tercios

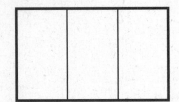

This shape has 3 equal parts.

These equal parts are called **thirds**.

The 3 equal parts are thirds.

thousand
millar

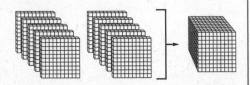

There are 10 hundreds in 1 **thousand**.

My Vocabulary Summary

V

vertex/vertices
vértice/vértices

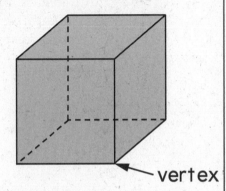

vertex

A corner point of a three-dimensional shape is a **vertex**.

vertex

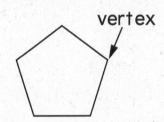

This shape has 5 **vertices**.

Y

yard
yarda

I **yard** is the same length as 3 feet.

© Houghton Mifflin Harcourt Publishing Company

My Vocabulary Summary

yardstick
regla de 1 yarda

A **yardstick** is a measuring tool that shows 3 feet.